PRIMITIV

I know this is all mere apparition compared to what awaits us, but it is only lovelier for that. There is a human beauty in it. And I can't believe that when we have all been changed and put on incorruptibility, we will forget our fantastic condition of mortality and impermanence, the great bright dream of procreating and perishing that meant the whole world to us. In eternity this world will be Troy, I believe, and all that has passed here will be the epic of the universe, the ballad they sing in the streets. Because I don't imagine any reality putting this one in the shade entirely, and I think piety forbids me to try.

Marilynne Robinson, *Gilead*

PRIMITIVE PIETY

A Journey from Suburban Mediocrity
to Passionate Christianity

Ian Stackhouse

Paternoster:
thinking faith

Copyright © 2012 Ian Stackhouse

18 17 16 15 14 13 12   7 6 5 4 3 2 1

First published in 2012 by Paternoster
Paternoster is an imprint of Authentic Media Limited
52 Presley Way, Crownhill, Milton Keynes, MK8 0ES
www.authenticmedia.co.uk

The right of Ian Stackhouse to be identified as the author of this work has
been asserted by him in accordance with the Copyright, Designs and
Patents Act 1988.

British Library Cataloguing in Publication Data

A catalogue record for this book is available from
the British Library.

ISBN 978-1-84227-786-7

Cover design by Phil Houghton
Printed and bound by CPI Group (UK) Ltd., Croydon, CR0 4YY

Contents

Preface

What it is that triggers the creative impulse in a writer is a question I find most fascinating. For some it is the location that inspires, for others a muse, and still others the silence of solitude. Speaking for myself, it has become clear over the years that I need the immediacy of the thing I am writing about in order to write, which in my case is the messiness of the church. To be sure, I crave the loneliness of the library in order to put what I am experiencing into words; but the initial spark, I am pretty convinced, is lit right in the middle of ecclesiastical chaos.

Certainly this was true of my first book: *The Gospel-Driven Church*. Even though it ended up as a doctoral thesis, in fact it was thrashed out amidst the very real pressures of being a young pastor and feeling that I was supposed to be raising the profile of the church, with all the nonsense that attaches to such an agenda. The book was my attempt to write my way out of a hole. Likewise, *The Day is Yours* was written against the backdrop of not coping very well with the increasingly ridiculous speed of life in the south-east of England, and was something of a cry for help if I am honest. I was writing in order to survive.

Primitive Piety came into existence in a similar manner. It was written in the context of what I now have come to see as something of a spiritual crisis. By crisis, I am not referring to my role as Senior Minister at Millmead as such, nor am I thinking only about Guildford. The thoughts and reflections in this book were gathering long before I arrived in Guildford. But it is probably true to say that arriving in the epitome of prosperous suburbia was the catalyst for the kind of primitivism that I am clawing my way towards in this book. There was something about the high-achieving, highly controlled atmosphere of this Surrey town – a town I love deeply by the way – that provoked a reaction in me almost from the beginning. The result is *Primitive Piety: A Journey from Suburban Mediocrity to Passionate Christianity.*

That this book has been three years in the writing is partly due to the demands of leading a large town-centre church. But in truth, the time lag is more because I have not been entirely confident about presenting my main thesis. After all, I am deeply a product of suburbia and some of the people who might feel most uneasy by what I write work very hard so that I can get on with the ministry. The last thing they need is my disapprobation. In fact, despite what might come across as a hard thesis, I love the people that form the Christian community at Millmead very dearly. In many ways they have been the answer to the questions I raise in this book and not the problem. I also remain deeply grateful for my evangelical heritage, and I hope I will still be considered by my readers as a strong proponent of it – especially after they read my chapter on the atonement (I am one of those rare evangelicals these days who actually believes in the more classical theory of substitutionary atonement). But now that I have read over the chapters one more time, I realise again that I have moved a long way from some of the cultural packaging that comes with modern-day evangelicalism; and I have decided to go into print about it because I believe that the church deserves something more gritty than our evangelical spirituality allows for, something more congruent with the drama that we see in the Bible.

I am aware, of course, that in the process of trying to do this – trying, in short, to deconstruct some of the cultural forms of contemporary Christianity – I am using the word 'suburban' almost as a synonym for what I see as its politeness, its tendency to cocoon itself from the real world. In that sense, I am using the word 'suburban' metaphorically. In doing so I am trying, in much the same way P.T. Forsyth did nearly a century ago, to describe a peculiarly effete form of Christian faith that has become the predominant expression in our churches. In so far as the church in this country is predominantly suburban and middle-class, then I guess it is an attack to some degree on that stratum of society, but it is not exclusive to them. In other words, one can be guilty of 'suburban piety', without living in suburbia. *Primitive Piety* is more an attack on cultural mediocrity than it is an attack on middle-class professionals.

There are a number of people I would like to thank in the process of writing this book. As always, I am very grateful to my very good friend Dave Hansen, whom I regard as one of the great spiritual writers of our generation. Catching up with him in Cincinnati during my sabbatical was wonderful. The many conversations we had over coffee, Graters ice cream, Skyline Chilli, as well as watching the Reds, were pure heaven. Thanks also must go to Karen Case-Green, as well as her husband Rob, who read the early draft chapters and made some very important remarks. She and I have collaborated on a number of things at Millmead over the years, ranging from poetry groups, preaching seminars, monastic spirituality, and the reading and singing of the Psalms. But alongside all of this, I am very grateful for her telling remarks on the pages of my earliest drafts. Indeed, only recently she pointed out to me Robert Alter's warning in *The Art of Biblical Poetry* about over-playing the primitivism of the Psalms.[1] As a matter of fact, Tom Howard warned me of the very same thing – what we might call an over-realised primitivism – in the many email correspondences we shared about the book. Indeed, it must be said that he remains uncomfortable about some of the sociology behind the book. But for his insights, his encouragement, his unbelievable gift for writing (he must surely be C.S. Lewis' natural successor), as well as the wonderful but woefully short twenty-four hours I spent with him and his family in Manchester-on-Sea, near Boston, I am also deeply grateful.

One of the surprises during the writing of this book has been the joyful reconnection with an old university friend, who in the intervening twenty-seven years or so since we last spoke has gone on to become an internationally acclaimed theologian. I knew Melissa Raphael at Durham. She and I and my room-mate Dean Sanders, who has also gone on to do some amazing things in his own sphere of work, spent many a pleasant afternoon discussing 'the meaning of life, the universe and everything'. Even then, she was using words in casual conversation that Dean and I, both grammar school boys, had never heard.

Why I mention Melissa here is because whilst she has been hugely encouraging about the general theme of the book, which corresponds in its own modest way with some of the themes she has written about in her extraordinarily rich tomes, she also took me on about what she regards as stereotyping when it comes to my reading of the Pharisees. As a Jewish theologian, not to mention a prominent feminist theologian, she is deeply concerned about the way Christians, and indeed the gospels themselves (texts which she has a deep respect for, by the way), tend to dismiss the Pharisees as legalists.

The issues she raises are too complex to be gone into here. Moreover, we have not had time to debate the issues properly. Therefore, with apologies to her, I have left those offending paragraphs unchanged. But what I do concede here is that I am aware that my use of the Pharisees for my own purposes is possibly a little anachronistic and that at times they are acting simply as a foil in much the way Melissa has identified. For this I take full responsibility and hope that the reader might interpret this as a heuristic device on my part rather than anything more sinister. I have a deep love for the Jewish people and am looking for ways to heal the hurts between Jews and Christians rather than exacerbate them. All I want to say is that any religious community, Christian community most of all, is susceptible to legalism – or more specifically what Marcus Borg refers to as 'the politics of holiness' – and that some of this at least can be discerned in the religious climate of first-century Judaism.

There are a whole number of other people who have been a great encouragement to me in the forming of this book: Susan Berry, David Bracewell, Rachel Burn, Andrew Burton, Jonathan Frost, Philip Greenslade, Ant Horton, Peter Jackson, Dora Jejey, Paul Ratcliffe, Stuart Reid, Roy Searle, Sara Sims, Tim and Charlotte Wears and Kate Kirkpatrick, of course, who has done such a great job of editing my random thoughts. I also want to thank the numerous colleagues in ministry with whom I have shared my thoughts on primitive piety over the years. The reception that my Baptist colleagues gave me, including one of my own colleagues, Rob May, when I presented some of these chapters at a retreat at Ashburnham, was most encouraging, and helped me to see that I had not completely lost the plot. At times I have wondered what was happening inside of me to cause such a deep reaction. But I am assured by my friends, and most of all by my dear wife Susanna, who bears the brunt of my existential angst, that whatever I am experiencing is worth going into print over. As always, Susanna retains my greatest thanks. Anyone who can live with a pastor, writer and frustrated missionary for as long as she has, and with as much grace, deserves a medal.

Before closing I want to say something about the cover of the book. For me, a book cover is very important, and signals to the reader something of the book's heart. This is particularly true with *Primitive Piety*, for it was while I was walking around Chichester Cathedral, paying my respects to my beloved Chagall stained-glass window behind the altar, that I spotted the exquisite maquette of 'Christ in Judgement' by the sculptor Philip Jackson. Almost immediately I began to see it as a religious image that drew together so many of the extremes that I was writing about: death and resurrection, suffering and joy, weakness and authority. I am deeply grateful to the Dean of Chichester Cathedral for giving me permission to use it for the cover of the book, to Judges and Sampsons Ltd in Hastings who released the photo image, and to Philip Jackson himself, of course, whose sculptures are simply stunning.

I am writing these words sitting in a very quiet study in my sister's house in Dollar, near Stirling, where she lives with her husband Leigh, and their two gorgeous King Charles Spaniels: Nina and Pasha. We have just had the pleasure of visiting our eldest son, John, at St Andrews, where he is studying theology. It looks like our second son, Timothy, will do the same. Both of them, as well as our third son, Benedict, are a great inspiration to me when it comes to writing. Our times around the table discussing matters of religion, politics and football, have been the richest blessing a father could receive. And when things have got a bit heated, or when I go on yet again about Owen Coyle's shock departure from Burnley Football Club a couple of years ago, it has been our fourth son, Daniel, with his winning temperament, who has calmed us all down. But it is to my sister, Deborah, with whom I started this paragraph, that I dedicate this book. She has been a big influence on my life, more than I have been able to convey to her, and furthermore a great support to me, in more ways than she realises. And if this book helps her to see through her antipathy to organised religion towards the real thing, namely a life of adventure in the kingdom of God, then I will be very happy indeed.

Introduction: Suburban Piety

> We tend them to a Christianity without force, passion or
> effect; a suburban piety, homely and kind but unfit to cope
> with the actual moral case of the world, its giant souls and
> hearty sinners.
>
> P.T. Forsyth, *Positive Preaching and the Modern Mind*

For reasons still unknown to me, sometime in the mid-seventies
my parents sent me to private school for a couple of years. Here
I was, a suburban junior school boy, weaned on a diet of *Saturday
Swap Shop*, *Football Focus* and *The Generation Game*, now making
his way along the silent corridors of a private boys' school. I
remember well the smell of the nearby school outfitters that we
visited, my father and I, weeks before starting at the school: that
peculiar, alluring aroma produced from the coming together of
polished surfaces, cotton rugby shirts, leather soles and tobacco.
And in my mind's eye I can still see our Headmaster lining us up
in the playground on a Friday morning to read out the names of
boys due to be caned on account of six black marks.

But whatever else school gave me, it was here that I began to
learn the English language. State schools in the seventies didn't
really teach grammar; we were taught to *feel* our way into it.
Instead of learning to conjugate a verb, we made it up as we went
along. So, as you can imagine, English lessons with the formidable Mr Lazenby were something of a nightmare. He was a
stickler for the subjunctive, relative pronouns and correct
spellings. I can recall losing a whole night's sleep worried about
the vocabulary test the next morning. But it was one lesson in
particular that stuck in my mind, and forms the burden of my

theme here. There we were, minding our own business, finishing off – I seem to recall – our English comprehension. Suddenly, from the heights of his pulpit-cum-desk, Mr Lazenby hurled a red-scorched script towards my desk and said these unforgettable words: 'Stackhouse, do not use the word "nice".'

Since that fateful day, I have passed through the old Eleven Plus, O Levels, A Levels, a university degree, Bible seminary and postgraduate studies to boot. Not only that, but I have composed countless sermons, and written a couple of books. But I defy anyone to find the word 'nice' in anything I have written (up to the present, of course!). It just doesn't feature. As Mr Lazenby impressed upon me, 'nice' is a nothing word. As they say in the north, it is 'neither nowt nor summat'; or to use the more familiar phrase: 'neither fish nor fowl'. Nice means mediocrity, nothingness, inanity. It is a word that falls to the ground as soon as you say it. Yet, it is just about the most apt word to describe Christianity as we know it. As Ian Pitt-Wilson puts it, summarising in one phrase all the preaching he had heard in churches in Southern California in the first six months of his time at Fuller Theological Seminary as professor of homiletics: 'It is good to be good, and nice to be nice.'[1] Or as one critic of the contemporary Christian scene put it, 'Blessed are the nice, for they shall see the kingdom of God.'[2]

One of the factors in the rise of niceness as the primary Christian virtue relates to the fact that the church in the United Kingdom, let alone Southern California, is predominantly suburban and middle-class. There is nothing wrong with this as such. It has taken me years to stop apologising for my suburban upbringing. But the trouble with middle-class Christianity, or certain forms of it at least, is that it tends to elevate its manners to the status of gospel. In the process vast numbers of people, characters, and emotions, are utterly excluded from the life of faith. 'The saints differ from us in their exuberance, the excess of our human talents,' notes Phyllis McGinley. 'Moderation is not their secret. It is in the wildness of their dreams, the desperate vitality of their ambitions, that they stand apart from ordinary men of good will.'[3] In the suburbs, however, we demonstrate a curious inhibition – and I am talking about the culture as a whole now – by which anything that fails to conform to a saccharine and increasingly self-indulgent sentimentality is deemed excessive.

This is not the whole story, of course. There is another side to suburbia, which can be every bit as colourful as the city. I recall browsing through a photo book in Waterstones once, the title of which I have not been able to track down since, which celebrated the more creative side of suburban dwellers. It was the conviction of the author that only in suburbia could you find such ingenuity, and that the juxtaposition of suburbia and soullessness was simply a myth. But whilst the pictures spoke for themselves, and did indeed represent a great deal of creativity, I failed to be convinced of the overall thesis. For whilst there is undoubtedly more under the surface of suburban living than meets the eye, and whilst middle-class people can be as radical as anyone in their approach to life, the pressure towards social conformity and cultural homogeneity makes this difficult to discern. Indeed, the emergence of suburbia in the late Victorian era was, by definition, an exercise in social conformity. As John Burnett explains, the suburban home had 'to proclaim by its ordered arrangements, polite behaviour, cleanliness, tidiness and distinctive taste that its members belonged to a class of substance, culture and respectability.'[4]

The theologian P.T. Forsyth, who features as something of a conversation partner throughout this book, actually uses the phrase 'suburban piety' to describe the kind of spirituality that I want to criticise here.[5] It is an interesting phrase, deriving no doubt from the fact that all five of his ministerial appointments in the Congregational church were in suburban locations.[6] But what it refers to in the world of Forsythian theology is that peculiarly effete, sentimental brand of late-Victorian Christianity in which the mysteries and the paradoxes of the historic faith are traded for the mood and sensibilities of polite society. In the suburbs of modernity, the location of my own pastoral ministry, many of the dramatic contours of Christian faith – death and resurrection, praise and lament, sin and grace – are eradicated, in favour of an ordered, attenuated religion that is no gospel at all. As David Goetz points out, in the setting of contemporary North America, 'Suburbia is a flat world, in which the edges are clearly defined and the mysterious ocean is rarely explored. Every decision gets planned out, like the practice of registering at retail stores for one's wedding gifts.'

So effective is suburbia at flattening the mystery, Goetz argues, that 'only tragedy truly surprises.'[7] Paradoxically, it is only really a tragedy that triggers good news – which leads us finally to relinquish the myth of control to a God who can truly save. Until then – and I am sure this is not exclusive to the burbs – faith is less urgent. Like Harry in John Updike's novel *Run Rabbit Run*, too many a modern Christian has 'no taste for the dark, tangled, visceral aspect of Christianity, the *going through* quality of it, the passage *into* death and suffering that redeems and inverts these things, like an umbrella blowing inside out. He lacks the mindful will to walk the straight line of a paradox. His eyes turn towards the light however it glances into his retina.'[8]

As someone who has lived almost his entire life in the suburbs, and ended up pastoring churches in relatively safe, low-crime areas, there is much in these descriptions that I recognise. Without wanting to reduce the congregation to a socio-economic category, for every congregation is infinitely more interesting and diverse than that, it seems fair to say that suburbia does a particularly good job in dulling the senses of faith. It is not as if the people themselves are dull. Under the surface all kinds of epics are taking place. It is more that the aspirations of a suburban lifestyle put a veneer on this. Jack Clemo bemoans this kind of piety in his poem *Outsider*: 'You miss the fire through your efficiency.' Indeed, these sophisticated people (though of course not everyone in suburbia can be described as such), 'are too sleek for a miracle,' because ultimately 'It takes/An unkempt faith to move a mountain.'[9] Real faith, as opposed to simulated faith, can only emerge, to use Clemo's stark, offensive language, from bare mud.

Clemo uses the word 'primal' to describe the faith he espoused; I prefer to use the word 'primitive', although not in the sense of a 'back-to-the-woods' kind of faith which is so popular these days among men's prayer groups, nor primitive in the sense of an idealised early Christianity, because it is quite clear that the early Church had its own take on congregational inertia. I mean primitive in the sense of stark: Christianity with all the angst left in; faith that is forged at the intersection of tragedy and triumph, rather than upon the criteria of being fun or boring.

In my experience, such a faith struggles to emerge in the suburbs. As I once heard Eugene Peterson describe it: 'Suburbia lobotomizes spirituality.' It rips the guts out of Christian faith; it renders banal the majesties of the revelation by turning them into the trivialities of itsy-bitsy religion. Forsyth evokes the subdued hues of the Sunday evening service as a way of describing the same: a strangely ahistorical, disembodied faith in which the historic Jesus of Nazareth is reduced to nothing more than an invisible friend; where the drama of dogma, to use Dorothy Sayers' image, is replaced by 'the promise of something nice after death.'[10] Primitive piety is my attempt to subvert this spiritual daintiness with something more angular: a piety that refuses to circumvent the language of sin, righteousness and judgement; that is bold enough to preach repentance when the world wants relevance; and, above all else, a piety that arises from the scandal of crucifixion and the surprise of an empty tomb.

Gritty Faith

Whilst travelling in Brittany a few years ago, I saw something analogous to this spiritual ruggedness in the work of the celebrated artist Paul Gauguin. Not noted for his religious piety, Gauguin nevertheless moved himself from Paris to Brittany on at least one occasion, for it was there among the church-going Breton peasantry that Gauguin found the primitivism that he was searching for in his art. Tired of the soft hues of the impressionists, and of what he considered to be their tame naturalism, Gauguin explored during his time in Pont-Aven a more symbolic style of painting in which non-naturalistic colours were employed to convey the more honest, rural piety that persisted in Brittany in such things as the annual pardons. He did not look on these annual rituals of collective forgiveness as a source of comedy, as did many artists from the city. On the contrary, Gauguin saw such religious ritualism, as well as the wrestling bouts that often accompanied these seasons, as a source of hope. Writing to his friend Schuffenecker, Gauguin explained his move to Brittany thus: 'You're a Parisianist. Give me the country. I love Brittany. I find in it the savage and the primitive. When my clogs ring out on this granite ground I hear the dull, matt and powerful tone I am trying to find in painting.'[11] Brittany, with its rugged coastline and its unsophisticated peasantry became a metaphor, which is why I refer to it here, of the holiness of the wild.

This call to the wild can itself, of course, become a cliché. Equating the rural with primitivism and the suburbs with conformity is not very original, I admit, and possibly something of a pastiche. But having acknowledged that point, it is undoubtedly the case that rural communities, often religious communities at the same time, preserve a grittiness of faith that seems to act for many artists, writers and poets as a prophetic challenge to the conformities of modern living. When William Blacker travelled to the north-west part of Romania and encountered timeless, although rapidly disappearing, peasant communities, he found it difficult to leave, for what he witnessed there was piety that was charming in its sheer particularity, even as it was disarming in its honesty. Speaking of his friend Mihai, an older man from an immigrant Saxon community, whom he grew to love as a father: 'He always took my part when others might laugh at my pretensions to living the peasant life, and when I would set off on my travels tears would roll down his cheeks. The people of the old Maramureş laugh and cry more easily than others. Nowadays, after thousands of years, life in the Maramureş is beginning to change. But as the world around them changed, Mihai and Maria remained the same.'[12]

Though we must not idealise them, these communities allow us suburbanites a window into the ancient and extreme world of the Bible. Here we are, in an increasingly homogenised world of modern living, where our emotional responses are increasingly manipulated by the media, when all the while the Bible beckons us into the strange world of the kingdom of God. Indeed, we must not regard conformity to the image of Christ as an exercise in emotional castration. That is to confuse Christian conversion with conformity to a certain kind of respectability (and, sadly, too much of this is offered up as the essence of spirituality). Rather, Christian faith is the celebration of holy eccentricity. It transfers us from the kingdom of blandness to the kingdom of the Son of his love, with all of its drama. After all, as William Kirk Kilpatrick points out, Jesus was hardly balanced: 'An individual reading the

Gospels for the first time without preconceptions for or against Christianity would not come away with the impression of a mild-mannered philosopher given to expressing His beliefs in carefully qualified opinions. To the contrary, the man seems as rash in His speech as in His actions. It is the language of heroes: sometimes crafty like Odysseus, sometimes bold like Achilles.'

As Kilpatrick goes on to say: 'He is given to calling people "fools" and "hypocrites." He indulges in fantastic metaphors about camels passing through a needle's eye. He makes inordinate boasts: "Destroy this temple, and in three days I will raise it up." He delivers stinging rebukes: "Are your minds so dull? You have eyes – can't you see? You have ears – can't you hear?"'[13]

Just so. Jesus is the very model of agitation. There is nothing balanced about him. Humble he may have been – a humility that he invites us to share – but never balanced, and therefore there ought to be more followers of this Jesus who give expression to this very same exuberance. Sainthood, as Michael Plekon points out, should be less an exercise in moderation – though it must include that at times – and more an experience of spiritual intensity. The models of our faith should not just be the sanguine types of our personality tests, but the melancholic, the immoderate and the mad. 'We need the example of these holy women and men,' Plekon says, 'who had no moderation but only exuberance. They were people with ordinary affections, who took God seriously and were therefore free to act with exuberance.'[14] And if they offend us, it is only because, to quote Chesterton, they are exaggerating what the world, and sadly what the church, has forgotten.[15]

A Dutch Saint

One of the saints Plekon holds up for our investigation is Etty Hillesum, a Dutch Jewess who converted to Christian faith a few years before she died in Auschwitz. To say she lived a colourful life is an understatement. Her voracious appetite for relationships with men, her moodiness as a young woman, and her unorthodox theology make her anything but an ideal candidate for sainthood. In a recent biography of Hillesum, Rowan

Williams cautions readers in his foreword not to take her morality as indicative of traditional Christian practice. As primate of
the Anglican Church I guess he is bound to say that. On the other
hand, he rightly, and bravely in my opinion, cautions us against
domesticating her life for the sake of Christian consumption, for
not only would this do her a grave injustice, but it would also
perpetuate the lie that holiness can only manifest within the safe
categories of conservative Christianity.[16]

The bottom line is (and maybe the following is a working definition of what a saint is): Etty Hillesum was a literalist.[17] For all
the ambiguities of her life, she took the words of Jesus seriously.
When Jesus said 'love your enemies' she understood this to mean
that every camp officer at Westerbork, where she served, was a
human being made in the image of God. And when the Bible
spoke of living with gratitude, she understood this to mean living with joy even in the midst of utter depravity. This is how she
lived, with an astonishing intensity, fuelled by prayer. And whilst
this in no way resolved the big questions as to why God allowed
the concentration camps, and in no way protected her from the
pain of it all, such intensity did mean that everyone who saw Etty
during those last couple of years testified to her radiance. She
presented the whole of her soul before the whole of human experience, and in this way became an icon of God.

Whatever else primitive piety is, in essence it is a return to this
kind of faith. Primitive piety is a protest, if you will, against the
blandness of so much suburban piety and an attempt to recover
the more radical side of faith – a radicalism rather like Richard
Yates tried to achieve in his prize-winning novel *Revolutionary
Road*, in which he depicts the attempts of April Wheeler to break
out of the cul-de-sac of 1950s American conformity and return to
the revolutionary spirit of 1776;[18] or a radicalism like Madeleine
Bunting's father tried to achieve when he left the ever-expanding,
homogenous, soulless suburbs of the South-East, and bought a
plot of land in North Yorkshire, complaining that in the suburbs
there may be comfort, but no splendour.[19] I offer *Primitive Piety* as
a similar critique of modern conformity: both an indictment of
certain strands of evangelical conservatism, with its obsession
with correctness, but also a vision of what Christian faith could
be, in the true spirit of propheticism.

That such a vision might be interpreted as the self-indulgent musings of a wayward Christian would not surprise me. I am already reconciled to the fact that for some *Primitive Piety* will seem to deviate from the norms of evangelical faith. But what I hope others will come to see is that the tendency towards perfectionism in evangelical notions of holiness is itself a deviation – as much an imposition on the biblical text as something that arises out of it. In fact, I would go further (and I would by no means be the first to draw this connection) and suggest that in this regard we are not unlike the Pharisees as they are presented in the New Testament, for like them we obsess over the minutiae of the law, when all the while we seem blind to the grand themes of justice and mercy. Anxious to preserve the exclusivity of life in the ghetto, we avoid getting our hands dirty in the messiness of the world. Hence our churches, as Forsyth once pointed out, are anything but gospel communities. 'We have churches of the nicest, kindest people,' he noted, but 'who have nothing apostolic or missionary, who never knew the soul's despair or its breathless gratitude.'[20] In other words, our reluctance to plummet the depths of our human failure means that we never get to experience the very thing that would send us out into the world: namely, the wonder of grace. All that we have to offer are the nicest, kindest people.

As someone who converted to Christian faith at seventeen, this is precisely what I began to observe. I discovered by my late twenties that in fact the kind of perfectionism that so much evangelical piety insists upon did not account for half the things that were going on in the deep recesses of my soul. At the risk of falling into one of those post-modern, post-evangelical paradigm shifts, I began to see that if I was going to grow, I may have to suspend my liking for the pristine, and engage with a spirituality that was far messier than I might like. Not only were the issues in my own life forcing me to accept this, life in the pastorate was requiring this of me too. Pastoral existence didn't present me with *ideal* lives, as I might have supposed, but *actual* lives: marriages that had gone stale, children that had gone off the rails, loved ones who had died in car accidents, women who ached with the pain of loneliness. So the choice was a simple one: either to read these lives through the lens of what ought to be, thus condemning them to the periphery, or listen to these lives as the raw stuff from which God was fashioning something beautiful for him.

Once I chose the latter and abandoned the former, then pastoral work became really interesting. It was not that I abandoned my Christian ethic, nor that I stopped offering directional counsel. That would have been disastrous. Rather, I no longer saw it as my job to fix people's lives. Instead, my task was to discern the workings of the Holy Spirit in lives that were as yet unfinished. What *Primitive Piety* seeks to explore is this egregious, and not so certain, terrain of Christian living. I try to articulate it here in the pages of this book in the confidence that even though it might be more messy, it will likely be more true.

In part one I seek to promote this in the place where so much platitudinous Christianity takes root: namely in worship. Beginning with the very heart of our worship, the cross and resurrection, I seek to articulate a theology of worship and prayer with all the awkward bits left in. Furthermore, I try to suggest in these opening chapters that whilst the criterion of relevance is not an entirely bad one on which to predicate Christian life and mission, nevertheless it has the effect of reducing the mysteries of the faith to something that we can control, rather than something we celebrate. As Edith Humphrey states: 'Worship should not be considered only in terms of relevance for today, or in terms of beautiful music and good aesthetics; rather, worship is entry. It is entry into something that is not primarily of our own making. Worship is entry into an action, into a company, into a reality that is on-going and bigger than we are.'[21] To state it in my own terms: worship requires us to let go of the controlled, risk averse environment that we have grown up in, jettison our distaste for extremes, and place ourselves entirely at the feet of the one who says, 'I did not come to bring peace but a sword.'[22]

Part two seeks to explore how primitive piety views human emotions. As one who has grown up within the evangelical tradition, I have become convinced that certain emotions are taboo, and that their prohibition often leads to disastrous consequences. After all, repressed emotions do not disappear; instead, they go underground, often to reappear at a later time in a more pernicious form. What I seek to demonstrate is the importance of recognizing the legitimacy of these passions – including human desire and sexuality – all the while mindful of the danger of simply indulging them.

Part three, then, considers primitivism in the context of Christian community and leadership. I want to ask: what would Christian community be if we allowed such primitivism space to flourish? What kind of organisation? What kind of leadership? For instance, we are used to seeing our leaders and politicians exercise great emotional restraint because, as former Labour party leader Neil Kinnock proved on more than one occasion, passion doesn't translate well on TV. But what if we permitted a different kind of leadership: one with all the emotions left in? What then? What would that do to our concepts of ordained as well as lay ministry? What would it do to our understanding of Christian mission?

In the final chapter I seek to articulate, by way of conclusion, a new vision of holiness: new, because rather than seeing holiness as the progress of the soul away from the raw stuff of our humanity, which is often how holiness is presented, actually it is quite the opposite. Our humanity is not negated by Christian existence; rather it is ennobled and brought to completion. As John Osborne puts it: 'If you can't bear the thought of messing up your nice clean soul, you better give up the whole idea of life and become a saint. Because you will never make it as a human being.'[23]

This says as much about Osborne's perception of religion, of course, as it does about his anthropology. As far as Osborne is concerned, sainthood is an exercise in avoidance of the raw stuff of our humanity. But what I hope to show in the conclusion, and in the book as a whole, of course, is that piety need not be so limp. If Christianity in the suburbs has become tame to the point of blandness, and holiness an exercise in social conformity, then our task in the chapters that follow, without ever compromising the moral vision of the church, is to make wild the holy, and holy the wild. I offer this call to holy wildness not as a disillusioned Christian, nor as someone who has ceased to be grateful for his past. The fact that I was converted in an evangelical charismatic context remains one of the great providences in my life. But if Christian faith is to remain a compelling force in our world, then it will need to break out of the straitjacket that this desire for correctness can sometimes impose, and explore a faith more rugged, even as it might be more biblical.

PART ONE

THEOLOGICAL PRIMITIVISM

One

Holy Love

Christian faith as I understand it, is not primarily a matter of signing on for the proposition that there exists a Supreme Being, but the kind of commitment made manifest by a human being at the end of his tether, foundering in the darkness, pain, and bewilderment, who nevertheless remains faithful to the promise of transformative love. The trouble with the Dawkinses of this world however is they do not find themselves in a frightful situation at all (unless, like myself, one counts Oxford High Table in that category), beyond the fact that there are a lot of semi-deranged people called believers around the place.

It is natural then, that they have no use for such embarrassingly old-fashioned ideas as depravity and redemption. Even after Auschwitz, there is nothing in their view to be redeemed from. Things are just not that desperate enough.

Terry Eagleton, *Faith, Reason and Revolution*

Just before Christmas 2008 Reverend Ewan Souter, vicar of St John's Church in Horsham, ordered the removal of the 10 foot sculpture of Jesus on the cross from in front of the church. Under pressure from local residents, as well as members of the congregation, the cross was deemed 'unsuitable' and too shocking for ordinary passers-by, and so he removed it, placing it inside the church instead. The task of the church, it was argued by the PCC, is to attract visitors; to make them feel welcome. The cross, depicting an emaciated Jesus, agony in stark iron, was putting them off.

The debate surrounding this decision to dismantle the cross outside a church is an interesting one, and by no means straightforward.

One could argue that it was just not good art. Indeed, it may well be the case that such a provocative piece of Christian imagery is better placed inside the church building rather than outside, thus giving people time to reflect on its meaning rather than scaring them out of their wits. Certainly, the group I discussed this with after church one Sunday felt that this would have been a better idea, and I am inclined to agree.

But that apart, it occurs to me that the decision of the parish council to finally give up on the cross is symbolic of a much more sinister movement in our churches, something tantamount to the sanitisation of Christian faith, the transformation of the brutality of the cross into something more palatable. Whether in the pulpit, hymns, or even at the altar, in the last two decades we have witnessed a massive failure of nerve in our churches over the central symbol of our faith: the cross has been neglected in favour of a piety that is altogether less scandalous. Concluding that the middle-classes are by and large too queasy to stomach the gory details of crucifixion, as well as the complex of sin and guilt that accompanies it, our churches serve up instead a peculiarly anaemic gospel where the cross is stripped of its offence, or simply ignored altogether. The situation is not much better in the academy. As Jürgen Moltmann notes: 'We have made the bitterness of the cross, the revelation of God in the cross of Jesus Christ, tolerable to ourselves by learning to understand it as a necessity for the process of salvation.'[1] It has become a formula rather than a passion.

It is this state of affairs that I want to challenge in this opening chapter of part one, not because I have a pathological liking for the macabre, nor even because I want to champion a particular model of the atonement, but simply because it has long been held that blood and sacrifice is central to the message Christians proclaim. If we want to effect a change in the piety of our churches, it must begin by embracing a more rugged cross. We may not want to push this exclusively in the direction of penal substitution. Clearly there are other metaphors for the atonement, equally as primitive and equally as valid. For instance, Joel Green and Mark Baker have made a convincing case for primacy of the *Christus Victor* metaphor in early atonement theology,[2] thus oxygenating what could easily become a stifling obsession with personal guilt.

Indeed, those who accuse conservative evangelicals of espousing wrath without love, or of serving up abstract, ahistorical religion, have a point. But what these same critics also fail to realise, often having traded in cheap caricatures, is that jettisoning concepts of judgement and wrath altogether rips the heart out of the gospel drama. Take the notion of judgement away from the gospel and we replace good news with simply nice news. Abandon notions of justice and holiness and love loses its steel. Accusing classical atonement theology of espousing a form of 'cosmic child abuse' may well be trendy, and to some degree justified, but in some ways what these theologians are doing is nothing more than what Marcion was doing in the second century: driving a wedge between the two testaments by pitting the God of love against the God of justice. For sure, there is a version of atonement preaching that is abusive: so devoid of love that Jesus is no more than a whipping boy for an angry God. But conversely, there are popular versions of the cross that are so devoid of holiness that the love ends up saccharine.

The fact of the matter is that love requires context. More specifically, the love of God in Christ Jesus requires the backdrop of judgement in order to understand it. As P.T. Forsyth put it – expressing his antipathy to late Victorian sentimentality – 'If we spoke less about God's love and more about His holiness, more about his judgement, we should say much more when we did speak of His love.'[3] For only then will we see love in its true colours. Clearly, the cross of Jesus Christ does not procure grace. This is not what Forsyth is saying. He would be the first to underline that the cross is the expression of grace, indeed flows from grace. All atonement theology and all gospel preaching should be predicated on the love of God. But for the love of God to be truly explosive, and not simply a synonym for niceness, holiness must be its origin.[4]

Quite clearly there are times when it is appropriate to interpret this grace as expiation of sin as opposed to propitiation; other times, to allow other images to dominate. Not all texts that seem to conform to classical notions of wrath and grace are actually so. But to suggest that simply by employing concepts of punishment one is perpetuating medieval, feudal notions of justice is equally fallacious. That God sent Jesus to be an atoning, even propitiating, sacrifice for our sins is not medieval jurisprudence but an important strand of primitive Christianity, and consistent with the portrayal of God in the Old Testament. It is there that we find notions of curse within the heart of the covenant itself, not as an expression of caprice on God's part, but as an expression of his love. As Frederick Buechner puts it, with reference to the prophetic judgement: 'a prophet's quarrel with the world is deep down a lovers' quarrel. If they didn't love the world they probably wouldn't tell it to go to hell.'[5] Not without reason did the prophets warn Israel of judgement with tears in their eyes. His judgements are an expression of his love, just as his love arises from the imminence of his judgements. Hence, when Jesus comes, in the fullness of time, to bear the curse of the law, we should not see this as some arbitrary piece of justice, less so a formula, as so often it is reduced to, but rather the climax of God's covenantal love. Luther didn't get it all wrong. He may well have read some of his Augustinian angst back into the text (and mistook first century Pharisaism for Romish indulgences to boot) but even so, Paul is not that far away from the theological angst of Luther's atonement theology when he says: 'God made him who had no sin to become sin for us, so that in him we might become the righteousness of God.'[6]

Whatever Became of Sin?

In order for this kind of primitivism to flourish once again in our suburbanised churches a bold restatement of some classic theological language will need to occur. The message of the cross is nonsensical without the words 'sin', 'guilt' and 'forgiveness'. But in the present climate of self-esteemism it is difficult to know how this might emerge without sounding retrograde. Sin has fallen upon hard times. It has been trivialised. Whereas the ancients spoke quite freely of the deceitfulness of the human heart and the need for atonement, these days most people associate sin with nothing more than an excess of chocolate cake. As Karl Menninger so memorably put it: *Whatever became of sin?*[7] One would be hard-pressed to find anything equivalent to Augustine's *Confessions* in the plethora of self-help books on the market. These days, pastoral appointments mostly take on the nature of counselling rather than confession.[8] As Eugene Peterson demurs, in his own pastoral reflections on the *Megillot*: 'Instead of attributing the suffering to the "sins of the fathers", it has assigned them to the neuroses of the mothers, and has put a whole generation of pastors to work in eliminating suffering from the soul.'[9]

In fact, so complete is 'the triumph of the therapeutic', to use Philip Reiff's phrase, that one wonders if there are any genuine sinners around anymore. We hear a lot about hang-ups, problems, neuroses; but whatever happened to good old-fashioned sin: sin that is hearty enough to elicit a saviour? In the manner of the infamous parlour-game in Dostoevsky's *The Idiot*, the confession of our worst sin before our circle of friends turns out to be no sin at all but mere peccadilloes; so trivial that all they do is present us in the best possible light. As Ferdischenko complains to the general, who begins the game by telling the assembled gathering of what he regards as his worst sin: 'And instead of telling us the worst action of your life, your excellency, you've told us one of your good deeds.'[10] Even pastors and priests seem to have colluded in this 'dumbing down' of sin. As Kathleen Norris notes, 'Pastors can be so reluctant to use the word "sin", that in church we end up confessing nothing except our highly developed capacity for denial.'[11]

The significance of this deceit for Christian faith is that by not disclosing who we really are, we rob ourselves of what salvation really is. One does not need to be a raving fundamentalist, nor subscribe to a particular view of the atonement, to acknowledge that the cross can only make sense in the matrix of human rebellion and divine salvation. Not to come clean about the impoverishment of our souls is to leave ourselves disenchanted concerning the greatest drama of them all. Again, we will be left with what Forsyth called those 'nicest, kindest people' who can run programmes but cannot make disciples because they have never known grace.[12] In other words, our churches lose their apostolicity to the extent that they lose their instinct for the basic gospel drama. Precisely because the believers within them have never really plummeted the depths of their own depravity, so they will never experience the astonishment of sins forgiven. Precisely because we refuse to face the bitter reality of self-centred living, all the time looking to circumvent the shame of the cross with a theology of glory, then we never get to taste the sweetness of a life restored.

Furthermore, there seems little hope of this situation changing. If suburbia is a journey away from the undesirables of the street towards the neat lawns of the cul-de-sac, then to admit one's inner mess, as we are seeking to encourage, is the soul having to make the journey back; but it is a journey that many are not prepared to take. We are happy to denounce social sins. The exposure of social sin, structural evil, economic injustice is something of a celebrity badge these days. But to make the journey into the labyrinth of one's own private sins, one's own private deceits, is just too much to face. Add to this an increasingly destructive media – savage in its treatment of even the most minor character flaws, constantly surprised by the ambiguity of life – and it is not surprising that there is a general reluctance in our society to speak honestly about anything. Apart from films or novels, where the honesty is far enough removed for it not to constitute a risk, most times there is a conspiracy of silence about the things that really matter. Whether we are dealing with heroes or villains, modern living has become increasingly vicarious.

This reluctance amongst moderns to confront the seedier side of our humanity has huge implications for the gospel. P.T. Forsyth again: 'We tend to a Christianity without force, passion, or effect; a suburban piety homely and kindly but unfit to cope with the actual moral case of the world, its giant souls and hearty sinners.'[13] Indeed, our culture's sunny optimism about human nature kills the church's message, since resurrection joy, by definition, can only properly arise out of an acceptance of the utter wretchedness of the soul. Contrary to what some might fear, this dialectic of sin and grace is not playing into the hands of an abusive, narrow, fundamentalist Christianity but simply to tell it as it is; to say what all primitive societies know, but which we in our squeamishness prefer to avoid: that what is needed is not a self-improvement scheme, but nothing less than new birth. As Kilpatrick somewhat wryly points out, with reference to our western utopianism:

> No actual 'savage' believes in the myth of the Noble Savage – or, if he does, he believes that all the noble ones lived long ago in the

Golden Age before the Fall, and he wishes he could be like them...Like the Christian, primitive man thinks there is something wrong with his nature. So in primitive societies, just as in Christianity, we see this desire to put away the old self and begin everything anew.[14]

Just so. The central symbol of the cross insists that we must cast aside the sensibilities that so often accompany pietistic faith and plunge headlong into the tragedy that is human existence. Whatever we think of Mel Gibson's *The Passion*, there is no doubt that it was a step in the right direction: an attempt to recover the sheer bloodiness of the drama. 'Without such a cross and its Atonement,' notes Forsyth, 'we come to a religion of much point but of no atmosphere, much sympathy and no imagination, much kindness and no greatness, much charm and no force – a religion for the well-disposed and not for the rebel, which we love our neighbour but not our enemy, and not our Judge; a religion for the sensitive but not for the world.'[15]

Indeed, as Forsyth goes on to say: 'Christ becomes a pathetic, tender, helpful and gracious figure rather than a mighty. We prefer the flavour of the evening service to that of the morning. The religion that is driven out of business and our energetic hours takes refuge in our tired hours and in our evening time. And it takes on that hue.'[16]

It is this state of affairs, he argues, that requires something more robust in terms of piety. In a climate where spirituality is very much in vogue, and where contemplative prayer has become something of a cottage industry, Forsyth urges us towards something more tenacious:

> What we need is not so much something pious but something positive which makes piety. We need fewer homilies upon 'Fret not' or 'Study to be Quiet,' fewer essays on 'the Beauty of Holiness,' or other aspects of pensive piety. And we need more sermons on 'Through Him the world is crucified to me, and I to the world,' or 'Him who was made sin for us.'[17]

Again, this is not the same as a 'Sinners in the Hands of an Angry God' kind of theology. God forbid. We must see wrath on the side of love. The fact that the prophets inveighed against Israel's sin, and warned her of dire consequences, was a sign that they cared. But care without a cross, compassion without crucifixion, and more specifically love without atonement, turns out to be nothing more than vague, disembodied piety. It is not the gospel that it purports to be. It ends up as a gospel for the well-disposed but not for hearty rebels. When von Balthasar began to articulate his distinctive theology of beauty, he recognised that for all our notions of glory, it must contain within it the note of crisis. 'If we fail to face the judgement of Christ,' he notes, 'every time we contemplate, we shall not perceive the distinctive quality of divine grace.'[18]

Easter Daffodils

Our cause is not helped by the way Easter is placed at the turning of the seasons. The occurrence of Holy Week at approximately the same time as the daffodils appear each spring plays right into the hands of sentimental piety, for it suggests that death and resurrection are no more than natural cycles in a trouble-free world. As winter passes into spring, so death passes inevitably into life. But as Dietrich Bonhoeffer reminded his congregation of German expatriates in Barcelona on Easter Sunday 1928, there is nothing inevitable about Easter, just as there is nothing natural about death. 'Good Friday is not, like winter, a transitional stage. No, it really is the end, the end of guilty humankind and the final judgement humankind pronounces on itself.'[19] In which case, as Bonhoeffer goes on to proclaim, Easter is something far more dramatic than we dare to imagine, for it speaks not of mere immortality but of resurrection: resurrection from a death that really is death, 'with all its terrors and horrors.'

My guess – as someone who regularly receives pious meditations on the back of funeral parlour brochures in the post – is that this is all too crude for twenty-first century mourners. Resurrection means we have to face up to death and reckon on its finality; and given our increasing unfamiliarity with death, if not outright denial, we prefer instead to think of death as 'nothing at all' and our beloved as 'only in the next room'. I understand this, and had better wait till I experience my own first major bereavement before I judge it too harshly. But what is behind it is a refusal to take seriously not simply the physical reality of death but also the theological reality of sin and judgement. The message of Easter is not that God takes already nice people and makes them nicer, hence the pretty daffodils, but takes condemned sinners and shows them mercy, hence the cross. And whilst we must ensure that this mercy of God is predicated on his love and not upon some arbitrary notion of justice, nevertheless to eliminate the language of sin and guilt altogether, as some are now doing, robs the cross of its real love, and thus its true glory. For his love is of a particular nature. It is *holy* love. It is love set in the context of holiness: God's holiness and our sinfulness. Indeed, in order to fully appreciate the depths of this love, one first must understand the threat of his judgement, lest love degenerates into mere sentiment.

That much of this sounds alien to our ears, if not offensive, shows how far we have moved away from primitive preaching of the gospel. For sure, there are other metaphors to describe the atonement, and possibly ones that are more apt in the present cultural climate. Again, those who warn against an overly forensic view of salvation raise an important concern. Not everyone comes to faith via the preaching of the law. But if we eliminate notions of sin and judgement altogether, as some now advocate, preferring instead a more psychological approach, not only will we rip out the heart of the gospel, we will also patronise our listeners with a gospel that is less than honest. For all our fears of fundamentalism (and they are very real fears), it is interesting to me that when Richard Mouw wanted to articulate something of the drama of the gospel, instead of employing the language of the academy – an academy that he has done very well by – he reverted to the unsophistication of his revivalist childhood and started talking once again about sawdust trials and altar calls.[20] My sense is that he did this because there is something about that crude, hillbilly fundamentalism that is closer to the gospel than our educated suburban theology. It may be uncouth, but take away the sawdust trail and we may well be serving notice on the death of Christianity within one generation. Writing about the earliest years of his own pastoral ministry, when theological sophistication was very much in vogue, Dave Hansen writes this: 'My faith devolved into a mild pantheistic pluralism, and I began to despise it. It was paltry, tooth-less. With the major paradoxes, like the doctrine of hell, taken out, my faith was as flabby as a week-old helium balloon. My ministry became futile and pathetic. I was of no use to anyone.'[21]

And so it is that the church must regain its nerve. As Sayers puts it:

> The dogma is the drama – not beautiful phrases, nor comforting sentiments, nor vague aspirations to loving-kindness and uplift, nor the promise of something nice after death – but the terrifying assertion that the same God who made the world, lived in the world and passed through the grave and gate of death. Show that to the heathen, and they may not believe it, but at least they may realise that here is something that a man might be glad to believe.[22]

Of course, the reason a man might be glad to believe it is because for all his suburban sophistication it is only the gospel, in its most primitive and crude forms, that is able to fully embrace the tragedy that is our humanity. The promise that *Love Wins* is all very well, and a comforting message for those who have had to find their way free of the bigotry of North American fundamen-talism, but in order for this love to be more than mere sentiment, it must be proven that *God Wins* too: that God triumphs over his enemies, destroys the power of sin, and raises us to life.[23] Anything less is not gospel. In fact, in his attack on the neo-atheism of Dawkins and Hitchins (who for the purpose of his Yale lectures get lumped together as Ditchkins), Terry Eagleton narrows down the debate to basically this: one between liberal humanism and tragic humanism. He writes that 'There are those like Ditchkins who hold that if we can only shake off the poison-ous legacy of myth and superstition, we can be free. This in my own view is a myth, though a generous spirited one. Tragic hum-anism shares liberal humanism's vision of the free flourishing of humanity, but it holds that it is possible only by confronting the very worst.'[24]

If Christianity is to thrive once more in the suburbs, it will need to confront this 'very worst', for only then will we understand why it is we call it gospel. Primitive piety, of the kind I am seeking to elucidate here, thrives on the polarities of faith: 'the one planted in divine sanctity,' to quote Romano Guardini, 'the other in the wilderness of sin. The Christian who surrenders these two points (the height and the depth of his faith) from which the vital tension of his Christianity depends, becomes more deplorable than the outright worldling.'[25]

I will argue in the next chapter that the recovery of these polarities is absolutely crucial if contemporary worship is not to descend into mere sentimentality. The polarities relate not only to sin and grace, but to a whole number of areas in our lives where instead of flattening the mysteries we are called now to embrace the extremes: repentance and forgiveness; holiness and love; cross and resurrection; and, to pick up on a much neglected theme, praise and lament. If suburban piety is uncomfortable with these paradoxes of faith, then primitive piety positively celebrates them. A more primitive kind of piety recognises that these tensions cannot be resolved so much as respected. To resolve them is to lose the mystery: to have everything answered; to reduce faith to a formula. To respect these tensions is to enter fully into the drama of Christian worship.

Two

Undiscovered Octaves

> But why is this music all so affirmative? Has it always been like that? Perhaps then a requiem, that glorious *German Requiem* of Brahms. I have to turn it off. There is too little brokenness in it. Is there no music that speaks of our terrible brokenness? That's not what I mean. Is there no music that *fits* our brokenness? The music that speaks *about* our brokenness is not itself broken. Is there no broken music?
>
> N. Wolterstorff, *Lament for a Son*

It is a truism that all cultures, all people for that matter, experience tears and joy and have ways of giving expression to this. My own propensity to tears comes, I am sure, from my immersion in Welsh culture from a very early age. If ever there is a nation that enjoys a good cry it is the Welsh – even when they are winning. As a child I can remember my mother crying along to the hymn singing at the Cardiff Arms Park as once more her beloved Welsh heroes, the holy trinity of Gareth Edwards, Phil Bennett and J.P.R. Williams, thrashed the English at rugby.

On the other hand, my roots on my father's side are in the north of England, which explains my lifelong support of Burnley (the sins of the fathers visited on the third and fourth generation); and just a few years ago, at the new Wembley, we celebrated their promotion to the Premiership after 33 years of languishing in the doldrums. It was one of the most cathartic experiences I have ever had. I said to my sons ten minutes before kick-off, 'I am going to really embarrass you in the next couple of hours.' But by the time the game was finished it was not just me who was singing. All of us were in a paroxysm of joy.

So there it is: weeping and laughter, praise and lament. In Israel these singing traditions were deeply intertwined. Contained within Israel's prayer book there were songs for all occasions: songs of thanksgiving, songs of trust, songs of praise and songs of lament. Indeed, the laments form a large bulk of these songs, which in itself ought to alert us to something about the rawness of Israel's story. But that aside for the moment, the point is this: Israel's worship gave expression – more often than not in a corporate setting – to the whole gamut of human experience. To use Walter Brueggemann's definition, Israel's worship was all about 'going to the extremes'.[1] There was nothing average about it. It was all or nothing. For sure, there were songs for when life was settled. We need those songs too. But since Israel's historical narrative proved so unpredictable, these songs – the spiritual equivalent of a musical *andante* – are few and far between. Most times Israel was either on cloud nine or down in the dumps. Most times it is either an *allegro* or an *adagio*.

This being the case, it is most interesting, therefore, and worthy of some comment, what Moses says to Joshua as they come down the mountain to confront what Moses already knows to be idolatry – what we refer to as the golden calf incident. Joshua tries to make sense of the noise at the foot of the mountain, thinking it is the sound of war, to which Moses responds, 'It is not the sound of victory, it is not the sound of defeat; it is the sound of singing that I hear.'[2] Or, to use John Durham's translation, 'not the sound of heroes exalting, nor the sound of losers lamenting, but the sound of random singing is what I hear.'[3] Gone are the vivid juxtapositions of celebration and mourning, the vivid memories of Israel's faith at the extremes. Instead we have just singing, tantamount to mere entertainment. In place of the grand sweep of Israel's story, sung about in the highest decibels of praise and the deep bass notes of lament, we have instead just singing that is neither here nor there.

I would not be the first person to comment on this, and I do so somewhat hesitatingly. But it occurs to me that the random singing that took place down in the valley on that day, lacking extremes even as it lacked a theme, bears striking resemblance to the middle-of-the road, easy listening of our own day. This is found in culture at large, but also, sadly, inside the church. As

Philip Greenslade puts it: 'In this loss of connection with the Living God in all his toughness and tenderness lies the seed of worship that is a mere singing of songs, a worship with no thought-out-sequence, that has lost touch with its vivid reasons for praise and lament.'[4] It is worship, as I have argued elsewhere, that can neither fully celebrate the gospel (because it has never grieved over sin), nor fully lament, because to do so would seem shameful in a culture which clings to its right to happiness. And so we have just singing: neither high praises nor soulish lament, but just singing; neither clashing symbols, nor weeping harps, just singing: happy songs for happy people with oh-so-happy lives.

It is a strange place to have arrived at, both culturally and in the church. We all know that life is not like that at all. Indeed, just below the surface of any congregation, however balanced, is a seething mass of dramas – as tragic as *King Lear* and as comical as *A Midsummer Night's Dream*. Our churches are Shakespearean theatres. You wouldn't think so. Judging by the faces of the people who present themselves Sunday by Sunday, and the ministry that is offered, you would think the congregation was a civic reception rather than a theatre. But as any pastor will tell you, even the politest faces conceal stories of epic proportions. And what the church needs is a liturgy that is commensurate with these grand narratives: worship that scales the heights and plunders the depths; that sings of his judgements as well as his grace; that sings of his grace precisely because it understands his judgements; that is reverent as well as joyful; joyful even as it is reverent.

My guess is that this kind of both/and worship – both liturgical and spontaneous; both tearful and festive; both reverent and intimate – will not be easy to recover. Our culture does not sit easily with such paradoxes. The church prefers not to do its theology dialectically. Whilst the Christian tradition celebrates the apophatic way, content to live with a measure of mystery and transcendence, our present church culture seems bent on eradicating such otherness, presenting the gospel in the happiest and most accessible terms possible. As Marva Dawn questions: 'Does our worship focus one-sidedly on comfortable aspects of God's character, such as his mercy and love without the dialectical balancing of his holiness and wrath? Is Jesus reduced to an imminent 'buddy' or 'brother' with the accompanying transcendence of God's infinite majesty?'[5] In my experience it does. Over the course of the last twenty or thirty years of renewal this is exactly what has happened. As one person quipped, 'we no longer worship God Almighty, but God Almatey.' I love what Annie Dillard says about all this:

> Does anyone have the foggiest idea of what sort of power we so blithely invoke? The churches are children playing on the floor with their chemistry sets, mixing up a batch of TNT to kill a Sunday morning. It is madness to wear ladies' straw hats to church; we should all be wearing crash helmets. Ushers should issue life preservers and signal flares; they should lash us to the pews. For the sleeping God may wake someday and take offence, or the waking God may draw us out to where we can never return.[6]

Religion as Relevance

Part of the problem, I believe, is that we have confused worship with evangelism. Nervous about the statistics on 'church growth' and the possibility, so we are told, of extinction within one generation, we have concluded that worship should be as much about relevance to seeker Harry as it is about reverence to Almighty God. But, of course, as soon as worship is assessed in terms of relevance, it is not long before our worship loses its glorious strangeness, its offence even, and carries the lightness of the world from which it came.

The architects of this kind of worship, where so much is hijacked on the agenda of cultural relevance, argue that this is what Wesley and others were doing: taking the songs of the taverns and inns and turning them into Christian music. But whilst there is some truth to this, no doubt, and whilst it is clearly true that Christian music can never, and must never, be culturally isolated, this approach seriously, and perhaps mischievously, ignores the deep resonances of the great tradition – Eastern Orthodox in particular – within Wesley's music.[7] In fact, I would argue it is only when we reclaim this great tradition, and not dismiss it, that the church will experience revival; for as often as not, as I have argued elsewhere, revival is not about the rejection of the past, but the recovery of it: a return to the sources – its cadences, its rhythms, its grand themes – so that we might better preserve our identity. By all means we should be contemporary. There is no virtue in antiquity *per se*. We need music that is recognisable. But always we must be able to descry when the liturgy bends to the needs of the listener, and ends up as just singing.

Worship is more than just singing. It includes confession, offering, preaching, reading, listening, pause, praying, and so much more. Indeed, one of the tragedies about the contemporary worship movement is that it makes worship synonymous with singing, hence the phrase – which really ought to be banned – 'the worship time'. Much as I love singing, and as much as I believe that the desire to lift up one's voice in praise is one of the hallmarks of New Testament Christianity, to reduce worship to just signing is a serious category mistake. It robs the church of those many other places in the liturgy where we encounter the Lord. It is to take the ancient liturgy, with its rhythmic movements of gathering, adoration, giving, intercession, hearing, thanksgiving, healing and blessing, and flatten it out into a medley of the latest songs.

Maybe in times of revival we can get away with this. When the Spirit comes, he can take whatever we offer him and turn it into a feast. And I am old enough to remember in the heady days of charismatic renewal when that was precisely the case. I remember times when the preacher could have preached about the virtues of an old sock and he would have elicited a response, such was the palpable sense of the presence of God. But I am also old enough to remember that those who conceived worship in those days, and even those who composed worship, were given to a far greater sensibility about what constitutes worship than is the case today, not only because they were more biblically literate, but also because they understood that the whole of what was offered in worship, in word, sacrament and prayer, was what constituted the gathering of the people of God. Communion was not a tag-on to worship, but the place where we came to give thanks for the great work of salvation; preaching was not something to be endured so we could get back to worship, but part of the worship itself – what Forsyth calls 'the organised Hallelujah of the church'; intercession was not something we did once in a while, but a regular part of our gathering together, the place where we called out to God for the world; the laying on of hands was not something that was offered willy-nilly, but a most serious proposition for those who hungered and thirsted for righteousness; and singing itself was something that was offered as a sacrifice of praise, whether the band was good or not.

This is not mere nostalgia. All these elements of the liturgy are still present in places of worship, whether Anglican or Baptist or whatever. The task at hand now, however, is to take these treasures of the church and polish them up: first, so that our worship does not degenerate into a musical repertoire; and second, so that if we do sing, our songs are high enough and deep enough to give expression to the whole range of human experience and emotion present in the congregation on any one Sunday. Christian worship should be joyful; of that there is no doubt. Joy is the signature of New Testament Christianity. But rejoicing in God is not necessarily the same thing as being happy about our circumstances, and if in the act of worship there are no octaves at the bass end, no minor keys, no discordant notes, then likely we will disenfranchise as many people as when we refuse to really celebrate. As Barbara Brown Taylor confesses, in her memoir of leaving church:

> One thing that had always troubled me was the way people disappeared from the church when their lives were breaking down. Separation and divorce were the most common explanations for long absences, but so were depression, alcoholism, job loss, and mortal illness . . . I was sorry that the church did not strike these wounded souls as the place where they could bring the dark fruits of their equally dark nights.[8]

This is because, in her words, our churches suffer from 'the full-sun effect': the pressure to put on a good face. Now that we are Christians, we assume that this is expected of us, and the liturgy reflects it. Ironically, in a community which apparently admits sinners, and which celebrates in communion the words: 'This is the blood of Christ shed for you,' we offer instead a peculiarly anaemic liturgy that pretends as if everything is alright.

But as Taylor admits, 'As enjoyable as it could be to spend a couple of hours on a Sunday morning with people who were at their best, it was also possible to see some strains in the smiles, the effort it took to present the most positive, most faithful version of the self.'[9] In fact, left unchecked, the effort required to pull off such a trick is usually too much, and people end up leaving church. But better than that, based on the wisdom that the one who cries is also the one who will be able to laugh, why not offer a liturgy that truly embraces our humanity, both the wintry and the sunny seasons of our lives? The joy expressed by our African sisters in our worship at Millmead, and which I have also experienced first-hand in West Africa, is not a device to avoid reality, or to hide tears. These women are familiar with suffering. They are as able to cry as they are to dance. So it is a joy that arises out of suffering, and a joy that thrives on the knowledge that despite our very worst sins, and our very worst fears, we are not consumed, because God's mercies are new every morning. As Nicholas Wolterstorff noted in his journal, following the death of his son, Eric, in a climbing accident: 'The Stoics of antiquity said: Be calm. Disengage yourself. Neither laugh nor weep. Jesus says: Be open to the wounds of the world. Mourn humanity's mourning, weep over humanity's weeping, be wounded by humanity's wounds, be in agony over humanity's agony. But do so in the good cheer that a day of peace is coming.'[10]

My dream is to inhabit a church culture where this kind of faith is not only permitted, but where it can thrive; where suburbanites overcome their very real timidity about being found out, see through the veneer that we present to one another, and foster a spirituality that is genuinely and distinctively Christian: that is, a spirituality that eschews sentimentality with its soft hues – as much as it eschews legalism with its harsh commands – and has the courage, instead, to live in the vortex of a faith that is dangerous even as it is compelling – a kind of Christian renewal, if you will, but one which insists that there is something grand about our worship. It is not a question of style, or even liturgical content, important as these are, but something even more fundamental, which must lie at the heart of all Christian worship: the fear of the Lord.

The Fear of the Lord

It was whilst preaching my way through the book of Proverbs a few years ago that I began to take seriously this phrase 'the fear of the Lord'. Just a quick Bible study will prove that it is a key theological term in this most practical of books. We know well the adage in the opening chapter of Proverbs that 'the fear of the Lord is the beginning of wisdom'. It is quoted again in 9:10 and then right at the end of the book in 31:30. But understanding the term is not as simple as rushing to the dictionaries to look up 'fear' and then 'Lord', as Eugene Peterson notes. The fear of the Lord is in fact one word – what in Hebrew we call a syntagm.[11] It is a hugely important word but one that is notoriously difficult to translate. None of the available synonyms in the English language seem adequate. In fact, when Rudolf Otto, a great scholar in these matters, analysed this core religious spiritual attitude, he found that nothing in his German language worked either so he resorted to a Latin phrase: *mysterium tremendum et fascinans*.[12]

Unless we know Latin, however, we are no further enlightened by this phrase than by the original one. So by way of illustration, let me take you in your imagination to Heathrow airport and park your car by the perimeter fence. A number of years ago I did so with my little nephew, Ted, who was about three years old at the time. We stopped the car, got out, and waited, just at the point where the runway ends and the planes fly over. We saw a few 737s, some Airbuses, then slowly, gradually, almost without us hearing it, we saw this great beast of a jumbo, climbing slowly off the runway just over our heads: a huge airplane no more than 200 feet about our heads. Ted in those days was a noisy little boy at the best of times, always chatting. But when he looked up and saw the jumbo, his little mouth quivered. He was silent. And stayed that way all the way home in the car. He had just experienced the fear of the Lord – that strange mixture of awe, terror, attraction, beauty, holiness, all wrapped up in one.

If that story doesn't quite do it, imagine yourself driving over a mountain pass, as we did a few summers ago as a family, crossing over the Logan Pass about 6,500 feet up – with incredible mountains ahead of you and a sheer drop to the left. If you are like me, you feel horror and beauty all at the same time. Part of you wants to hug as close as you can to the mountain; another part is drawn inexorably towards the edge. It is what we call the fear of the Lord. Only this time it is not a jumbo jet, or crossing the Rocky Mountains: it is Sinai, Mount Tabor, Golgotha – that place where, as Graham Kendrick says, 'wrath and mercy meet'; where we shrink back in terror at the enormity of our sin and the judgement of God that the Son of God should die; and at the same time, without ever losing our sense of reverence, drawn with wonder at the mercy and forgiveness contained within the cross for all those who put their trust in him. That is the fear of the Lord. As John Newton put it in that immortal hymn: 'Twas grace that taught my heart to fear, and grace my fears relieved.'

The point of these two illustrations is to underline the fact that Israel's faith was, at heart, primitive. Yes, it was practical. What is the book of Proverbs but the most practical book in the whole of the Bible? And yet the praxis was rooted in the worship of a God who could inspire love and fear at the same time. Theologically we might express it this way: their worship held together what we in Christian renewal so often put asunder, namely transcendence and immanence, God's otherness as well as his nearness. And in my opinion, unless we recover this sense of the fear of the Lord, then we are done for. All our Christianity will amount to will be a sloppy kind of sentimental religion, where it doesn't matter if we mess around because 'God will forgive'; it will provide nice ideas on how to be a decent person – rules taught by men as Isaiah 29:13 puts it – when what the Bible calls living with wisdom has the fear of the Lord at the centre: reverence, dread, awe, respect, humility – *mysterium tremendum*. The *mysterium tremendum* is the beginning of wisdom. You are not at the centre of the world; he is. To put it bluntly: shut up. Stop messing around in trivialities and banalities and pay attention.

Lest we become overly mystical in our worship, the fear of the Lord in the Bible is something very practical. The man who puts controls on his computer, or regulates his night-time viewing, or asks for accountability, or keeps a watch on his tongue, or watches his credit card account, is someone who is living in the fear of the Lord. The woman who dresses modestly, or refuses to gossip about other women, walks away from a potential affair with a colleague in the office, or teaches her child to care and not bully the odd child in the playground, is someone living in the fear of the Lord, precisely because as Proverbs 14:27 puts it: 'The fear of the Lord is a fountain of life, turning a person from the snares of death.'

However, this approach is not to be confused with law. It's what you might call affectionate reverence: not wanting to offend him because, as Paul says to the Ephesians, that would be to grieve the Holy Spirit of God who is in us and who has given us such life.[13] Indeed, we see the same thing in Moses. Just like Moses said to the people God rescued out of Egypt and before they crossed over into the promised land: 'Oh that their hearts would be inclined to fear me.' He says this in Deuteronomy verses 5:29, 6:2, before the famous declaration in 6:4, 'Hear O Israel, love the Lord your God with all your heart.' There it is: fear and love all mixed up together. We believe his promises and so love him; and we believe his threats and so fear him.

There are those who say that such primitivism diminishes by the time we get to the New Testament: that instead of the God who slays an Uzzah for touching the ark, we encounter a God who wouldn't say boo to a goose – a kind of latter-day Marcionism, where all the nasty bits are excised. But this only proves one thing: these people have never read their New Testament properly. For sure, we have not come to Mount Sinai, says the writer of Hebrews, 'to darkness, gloom and storm.' Instead, we have come to Mount Zion, 'to the heavenly Jerusalem, to the city of the Living God.' But just when we think it is safe to get back in the water, chill out a bit, put on some smooth classics, and have a chat with God, the preacher goes on to say that 'since we are receiving a kingdom that cannot be shaken, let us be thankful, and so worship God acceptably with reverence and awe, for our "God is a consuming fire".'[14] In other words: grace does not diminish reverence; it intensifies it.

Again, whether our present suburban religion can sustain such paradoxes of faith, such tensions, such existential angst, is a moot point. Suburban piety flattens out paradox; it is uncomfortable with angst; it would prefer to play safe than live with fire, or if it did get passionate, would do it like some religious striptease. But it is not a new enthusiasm we need, nor a new piety, but a recovered Word:

a Christianity that can live with extremes: a faith that is both liturgical and spontaneous, tearful and festive, ancient and future, and finally, since the fear of the Lord is the beginning of wisdom, a faith that is reverent and intimate, without ever needing to resolve the tension.

Ratty and Mole

In closing, there is a scene in the well-known children's story, *The Wind in the Willows*, which wonderfully points to what we are after. Some way into the story, Rat and Mole are about to retire for the night, when Rat mentions to Mole that the young otter, Portly, is lost. So giving up their sleep they go upstream in the boat, in the light of the silvery moon, to find the little rascal. All of a sudden, Rat is gripped by the sound of this most exquisite music. At first Mole can't hear it, but then he can, and the two row in the direction:

> 'Row on, Mole, row! For the music and the call must be for us.'

And there on a small island they encounter this august presence, still holding the pan-pipes that had produced the wonderful sound, and little Portly sound asleep, peaceful and content nestling between the hooves.

To this day, I haven't met a *The Wind in the Willows* lover who knows where this comes from. It is a chapter that comes completely out of the blue. One wonders if Kenneth Grahame was a Christian, because then he writes:

> All this he saw, for one moment breathless and intense, vivid on the morning sky; and still, as he looked, he loved and still as he lived he wondered.
>
> 'Rat,' he found breath to whisper, shaking. 'Are you afraid?'
>
> 'Afraid?' Murmured the Rat, his eyes shining with unutterable love. 'Afraid! Of *Him*! O, never, never! And yet – and yet – O Mole, I am afraid.'
>
> Then the two animals, crouching to the earth, bowed their heads and did worship.[15]

As I read this passage from *The Wind in the Willows* one last time to my youngest son, Daniel, having read it one time or another to each one of his older brothers when they were his age, it occurred to me that the worship of Ratty and Mole, albeit to some riverside deity, encapsulates what we are after here: relief after a great anxiety; thanksgiving for the mercies of God; joy that our prayers have been answered. But above all else, it describes the terrifying yet utterly compelling beauty of holiness:

> Worship the Lord in the beauty of holiness.
> Bow down before Him, His glory proclaim. [...]
> Mornings of joy give for evenings of tearfulness,
> Trust for our trembling, and hope for our fear.[16]

Three

Honest Prayer

Engine against th'Almightie, sinner's tower,
Reversed thunder, Christ-side-piercing spear.

George Herbert, *Prayer*

I don't quite remember when it happened, but there came a time when I sensed that God must be getting bored of my prayers. If I tire of hearing polite, perfunctory prayers, then how much more does God tire of the dull platitudes of my own praying? It was time to take the plank out of my own eye and be more honest – the kind of honesty Stanley Hauerwas developed in his prayers during chapel at Duke University and which his students, who possibly had never heard such candour in church before, persuaded him to publish. The one I like the most, and which I have quoted in numerous different settings, goes like this:

> Zealous God, we confess, like your people Israel, that we tire of being 'the chosen'. Could you not just leave us alone every once in a while? Sometimes this 'Christian stuff' gets a bit much. Life goes on and we have lives to live. Yet, unrelenting, you refuse to leave us alone. You are, after all, a zealous God. You startle us from our reveries by gathering us into your dream time, into your Church. May we, thus gathered, be so inspired by your Spirit that our lives never tire, that we have the energy now to wait, to rest, in the goodness and the beauty of your truth. Amen.[1]

Why I love this prayer is because I have felt this, and I know many in my congregation have felt this way too at times. I know this because they tell me. It all just seems too much. Trying to be holy, seeking to do the right thing, living out of my will, is hard work. But until I read Hauerwas, I don't think I had the words nor, to be honest, the guts to articulate it, neither for myself nor for my congregation. I wasn't sure if a pastor was permitted to pray such a prayer, which is odd, because as soon as I did, as soon as I decided one Sunday to actually read this prayer out, it was met with universal relief – a relief which I also observed when I read the following prayer out a couple of weeks later. The prayer comes from the same collection as the previous one and is set, as Hauerwas puts it, in the context of 'a particularly egregious act by a member of the divinity school that brought shame on the school.' It goes like this:

> Weird Lord, you never promised us a rose garden, but right now we could use a few daisies or zinnias. We feel confused, unsure of where we are, angry because a wrong has been done and we are unsure who to blame. It ought to be somebody's fault, but even the one who is to blame is so pathetic it hardly seems worth the effort. So we are left with ourselves. Work on us to make us a community of truthfulness, a community where friendships flourish, a community of joy in the work you have given us. Help us to know how to go on, confident that you have made us characters in the best story since creation, since it is the story of creation. It is good to be your people. Amen.[2]

No wonder Hauerwas' students wanted these prayers published. They are honest prayers, based on the maxim that one should 'pray as one can, not as one can't'. In fact, in his memoirs Hauerwas notes that his fundamental rule in writing these prayers 'is never to think that my job is to protect either God or us from the truth.'[3] The idea that we should 'just ask you, Lord' was anathema to him. Discreetness is still a virtue, to be sure. Honest praying in public is no excuse to hang out all the dirty laundry. Indeed, there is most definitely a difference between public and private prayer. But even so, Hauerwas encouraged me to gamble on the possibility, even in the more public context, that since God knew what was in my heart in the first place there was no point in hiding it from him in my praying. I may be able to pull the wool over my own eyes, and even the eyes of the most skilful mentor, but I certainly couldn't pull the wool over God's. Better an impious prayer that was honest, than a pious prayer that was dishonest.

This is right, of course. What is prayer but primary language; primordial emotion; primitive groaning? We have language to achieve things, language to motivate, language to inform. As we grow older and more sophisticated, we learn this secondary and tertiary kind of language because it helps us to get on. But in prayer, as Eugene Peterson reminds us, we return to primary language:[4] longings, sighs, mutters, inarticulate groanings of the Spirit, as the apostle Paul calls it, that echo of the huge subterranean groanings of a frustrated creation.[5] In short, prayer is not our way of proving our piety to ourselves and to others. That way lies death. Instead, like poetry, it is an attempt to wrench to the surface and present to God what lies most deep and most essential, in the hope that somewhere in the struggle of the whole thing we will get a blessing. To use a very primitive image from the life of Jacob, prayer is wrestling. Put aside images of pious mediations down by the lakeside, a soft lens, coffee-shop posters of lush pastures and the text 'Be Still' – though there is no doubt that these have their place. Prayer is Jacob wrestling with the angel;[6] it is the widow beating the judge until she gets justice;[7] it is the friend at midnight making a nuisance of himself until he gets what he wants;[8] it is little Epaphras, somewhere in the Lycus valley, struggling in prayer for his fledgling converts,[9] and in this way mirroring his Lord who spent a whole night in the garden wrestling with his Father.[10]

There is no virtue, of course, in this kind of praying. Books that exhort us to pray long and hard, battering down the gates of heaven, often do so in such a way that prayer is presented as a virtue. That is not my intention here. My intention is quite simply to say that this is what prayer is: honest speech. As Dave Hansen puts it in *Long Wandering Prayer*: 'In God's presence we may need to remove our shoes and fall on our face, but when the talk begins we need to get into God's face.'[11] Indeed, one of the reasons I preached through the book of Lamentations one Lent was to inculcate in the congregation precisely this kind of thing: just that ability to pray our complaint.[12] For sure, the guilt is real. Unlike the book of Job, the poet of Lamentations knows that

Israel is guilty of multiple disobediences and, in one sense, deserves everything she gets. Lamentations is a confessional, whatever else it is, and therefore entirely appropriate as a Lenten text. But the fact that Israel quite clearly feels that God may have overdone the judgement thing means that a preaching series in Lamentations also tutors us in the way of complaint. 'Is any suffering like my suffering, that was inflicted on me?' asks the poet.[13] 'Look, O Lord and consider: Whom have you ever treated like this?[14] Why do you always forget us? Why do you forsake us so long?'[15] No answer is given, of course. But by giving voice to the question, scripture legitimates just about anything we might want to say in prayer. Piety insists not only that we confess but also that we complain, not simply that we petition but also protest.

North and South

That we don't pray this way says a lot about our middle-class sensibilities. Suburbia tends not to permit such rawness. By definition suburbia is about the circumvention of honesty. Indeed, the word 'suburbia', for many people, is synonymous with Home Counties' politeness. If in the north of England you call a spade a spade, in the south, to change the metaphor, we go round the houses. We southerners devote so much time avoiding the real issue that likely as not we will never actually say what we really want to say.

Carried over to the pastoral setting, this makes for very dull visits indeed. Who wants to drink cups of tea with parishioners simply talking about the weather? In fact, by the time someone plucks up the courage to tell it as it really is, often it is time to go. But not always. Not even the suburbs can arrest the ravages of time. We may want time to stand still, take a photo of our immaculate lives, but sooner or later life happens. Not even Christians are immune from this, whatever the smiley preacher says. A fifty-year-old man loses his job without the prospect of another; a wife walks out on her husband of twenty years; a teenage child gets knocked over by a car; a little two-year-old dies of cancer; an aging father gets Alzheimer's. Then, all of a sudden, in this place of rawness, we find ourselves praying. In fact, we pray for what feels like the first time, as I did when my father was rushed into hospital for an emergency operation. We throw caution to the wind, suspend all pleasantries, and pray from the guts.

As a pastor, I have the privilege of getting close to some of those prayers. And what I discover, almost every time, is that the person concerned would not trade this new-found immediacy in prayer for anything. For sure, the situation is desperate. Like the psalmist, we cry: 'O for the wings of a dove,' so that we can fly away;[16] or failing that, try to hope against hope. As Dylan Thomas once put it, with reference to the perpetual greyness which is South Wales: 'I take walks in the morning and pretend there's sun in these disappointed skies.'[17] Once the awful reality of the situation is accepted, however, it is as if the person discovers prayer for the first time, or at least the kind of praying that the Bible bears witness to: primitive, gutsy, intense praying that continues even when the sun does eventually come out to play, furnishing now our praise where it once served for our lament, only this time deeper for the experience.[18]

To those looking on, such praying and such people may seem a bit extreme and not readily understood. 'Listen, he's calling Elijah,' they said of Jesus' cry of dereliction from the cross.[19] But that is exactly the point. Prayer is extreme. There is nothing moderate about it. And to argue for the supremacy of balance over and against extremes – in the way that some castigate Pentecostal piety for its rawness and lack of balance – is, as Steven Land points out, nothing more than ecclesiastical snobbery.[20] Though we may want to question certain expressions of extremity as little more that hyper-spirituality, nevertheless, for all our liking of measured and average men, those who pour out their hearts *in extremis*, in both praise and lament, have the Bible on their side. Fat Eli may want to ridicule Hannah for her indelicate piety, but in the end it is Hannah who is heard by the Lord, and Eli who fumbles around in the dark.[21] For piety, as in fact Eli comes to see, is not tidy any more than it is mere enthusiasm. Indeed, enthusiasm can often be the enemy of true prayer – nothing more than affectation. Rather, true piety is the pouring out of one's whole personality, one's whole soul to God, in the knowledge that until one has prayed with the whole of one's person, given up on the project of self-deceit, and laid out one's soul bare before the Lord, one has not prayed at all. As John V. Taylor puts it:

> What God loves is nothing but the whole – the whole self in the whole situation. That and nothing else is what is present to God; all present . . . this entails calling in one's self from the past, the regrets, the resentments and scars, and presenting them to the eyes of his love. It entails calling in one's self from the future, the day-dreams, the fears, the ambitions, and presenting them, leaving them with him. It entails calling in the self from beyond the pale, the self that would properly be banned from one's autobiography but is a true part of the one God loves.[22]

This kind of praying takes a lot of courage. It requires a lot of faith. In order for such candour to take place it requires a conviction that it is indeed better, as David said, to fall into the hands of God than into the hands of men.[23] But once we believe that – as surely we must believe if piety is to emerge as anything more than suburban – then prayer becomes the ultimate exploration of the self, since it is spoken before the face of the one in whom we live. Prayer becomes the most essential way in which the Spirit can properly claim to have taken possession of us. Again, Hansen: 'God does not require polished theology or flawless faith in prayer. But God may well require a total outpouring of body, mind and soul in prayer as the act of loving him with our body, mind and soul.'[24] It is only when God has all our tears, and all our hollering, and all our arguing, and all our reasoning, that it can be said that God has all of us.

Extempore Prayer and Liturgical Prayer

This insistence on honesty is not a defence of extempore prayer, by the way. Liturgy can achieve this just as well as charismatic spontaneity, and at times more so.[25] Indeed, we have a whole range of liturgical prayers in our Psalter that tutor us in this kind of candour, of a kind that would be distressing to most suburban congregations. For instance, when was the last time you heard a pastor praying that God would dash the children of his enemies against the rocks?[26] According to the terms of my contract, and given the present climate of fear concerning child abuse, I could lose my job for that kind of brutalism in the sanctuary. Yet there it is in our psalms: what we call, in our desire to label everything, imprecatory psalms. And precisely because it is there, we have to pray it, when otherwise, left to ourselves, we might conclude that such vituperation is not permitted for the people of God. Liturgy allows, where spontaneity avoids.

The same is true for a whole range of emotions. Since the psalms are, to use Calvin's phrase, 'an anatomy of the soul', expressing everything from high praise to deep lament, then simply by adhering to the routinised praying of the psalms one is likely to give expression in just one month to all manner of feelings which, left to our pious selves, we would be unlikely to own at all – not in a year, nor even in a lifetime of Christian prayer. It is no coincidence that when the bottom does indeed fall out of a person's life, as I have observed numerous times among the people I live with, it is to the psalms that these same people turn. Psalms, for all their liturgical fixity, are perfect for pouring one's heart out to God. Psalms encourage primal emotions precisely because they are formed within liturgical prayer forms. When a dear friend of mine went through the agony of his wife leaving for another man, it was to the psalms that he instinctively turned; when a church leader I knew went through a nervous breakdown, it was the psalms he discovered as his closest companion; when a friend of mine went through the most tortuous two years, not sure if she could carry on with her life, it was the psalms that kept her alive. As Anne Michaels puts it in *Fugitive Pieces*, 'Grief requires time. If a chip of stone radiates its self, its breath, so long, how stubborn might be the soul? If sound waves carry on to infinity, where are the screams now? I imagine them somewhere in the galaxy, moving forever towards the psalms.'[27]

The Psalms achieve this because, like us, their language is often fragmentary, if not downright contradictory. For instance, as Hansen points out, Psalm 55 moves from escapism, to vengeance, to trust all in the space of twenty-three verses.[28] How like us. One moment we want to flee to the wilderness, the next minute to strike our enemies on the jaw, and the next minute to cast our cares on the Lord because he cares for us. And precisely because the psalms give expression to these mood swings, accurately reflecting what most likely formed over a few weeks rather than in the one minute it takes to read, they become our tutors in the way of self-disclosure, helping us to expose to the light of God every chamber of our lives and not just the tidy ones. We may well get to the point where we cast our burdens on the Lord. Peter picks up this command and places it right at the end of his first pastoral letter.[29] But often it takes a good number of flights of fancy, plenty of self-generated vengeance and not a little self-pity before we get there.

Pray without Ceasing

It may well be that this kind of praying, of the long wandering kind, is what Paul is thinking of when he exhorts the Thessalonians to 'pray without ceasing'.[30] To pray without ceasing is not so much round-the-clock devotion as much as it is a bent of the soul that is constantly returning to God with the actualities of our lives and the situation we find ourselves in. Sometimes it is conscious prayer. Oftentimes it is subconscious, underground muttering as we attend on the surface to the mundane everydayness of our lives. But always it is the inclination of the soul towards God, withholding nothing from him, however messy, in word and thought and deed.

That we learn this kind of praying on the anvil of suffering is usually the way it begins; that we continue to pray this way is essential if our suburban piety is to develop into something beyond sentimentality and quietism. Churches in suburbia are facing a crisis of faith, a crisis of prayer. Our prayers are effete, dishonest, stoical, fatalistic. Too quickly, as Forsyth was at pains to point out, do we pray the prayer of resignation 'Thy will be done', thinking this is spiritual, when for Jesus, as indeed for Paul and his thorn in the flesh,[31] this utterance came not at the beginning but only at the end of the struggle.[32] Our fatalism mirrors that of David's servants following the death of Bathsheba's bastard child. Puzzled that David should get up from prayer, wash and eat, now that the child is dead, David, on the other hand, sees it as entirely logical. 'While the child was still alive, I fasted and wept. I thought, "Who knows? The Lord may be gracious to me and let the child live." But now that he is dead, why should I fast. Can I bring him back again?'[33]

In other words, while the rest of us deliberate over whether it is right to pray for healing, whether indeed healing is God's will in this situation – and in the process end up doing nothing – David, ever the opportunist, simply assumes that it is God's will. Until he hears otherwise, as Luther would put it, he takes a joyous wager on the unseen, unknown goodness of God. Prayer for David was not a theological proposition: something you do when you have worked it all out. If that was the case, he would never have prayed. Rather, it was something you did because you had to, leaving God to work out the theology.

I love David for this. After all, who knows why God allows suffering? Who knows why some people get healed and others don't? We may take a stab at answering it, but in the end it is a theodicy. What David insists on, however, is that the theodicy must never become an excuse for prayerless fatalism. Forsyth again:

> Let us beware of a pietist fatalism which thins the spiritual life, saps the vigor of character, makes humility mere acquiescence, and piety only feminine, by banishing the will from prayer as much as the thought has been banished from it . . . the popularity of much acquiescence is not because it is holier, but because it is easier. And an easy gospel is the consumption that attacks Christianity.[34]

Better to pray and not see our desires, than not to pray at all, for it may well be that prayer is its own answer. After all, for all the books written on prayer, and all the various sophistications of prayer, it appears that the sum total of what Jesus taught about prayer is simply to keep on asking, keep on seeking, keep on knocking.[35] Surprisingly, the primitive and not particularly polite attitude of importunity is at the heart of Christian piety. This is not because God stands at some distant place, unable to hear the cries of his people. Whatever else the parable of the unjust judge teaches us, it teaches us that God is precisely not like an unjust judge: 'Listen to what the unjust judge says. And will not God bring about justice for his chosen ones who cry out to him day and night?'[36] God is our Father, and he is willing. And yet, somewhere in this elective, filial love, there is this 'crying out to him day and night.' Quietism and resignation may well form the basis of many of our contemporary praying traditions, and feature highly in our retreat centres. Contemplative prayer is now something of a cottage industry. But as far as I can work out, the very highest of Christian prayer and Christian intimacy – or at least in no way inferior – appears to be crude, rugged insistence. 'Does not Christ set more value upon importunity than on submission?' asks Forsyth.[37] He does, and there is nothing pretty about it. It is Abraham haggling with God over the fate of Sodom and Gomorrah – 'What if there are fifty righteous people in the city?';[38] Moses flattering the Lord to repent over the fate of rebellious Israel – 'O Lord why should your anger burn against your people, whom you brought out of Egypt with great power and a mighty hand?';[39] David manipulating the Lord to spare his life – 'Who praises you from his grave?'[40]

And yet, all the while the sovereignty of God is never in question because we sense that this dialogue is taking place in the heart of God himself. That is, the only reason Abraham can seemingly *haggle* with God for mercy, not justice, is because it is in the heart of God that his mercy triumphs over his justice. The only reason Moses can appeal to the honour of God's name to spare the Israelites is because God has already signalled in so many words his desire to relent from judgement. And the only reason David can seemingly manipulate God towards a dramatic recovery of health is because, in the future, resurrection will be the primary way that the Lord will disclose his true nature as the God of life.

In other words, prayer is God answering God. It is frail humanity caught up in the great soliloquy in the heart of God. Put aside dainty prayers and self-conscious sentimentality; prayer is glorious self-forgetfulness as we get caught up in the birth pangs of the new creation. Just as the creation groans, as in the pain of childbirth, waiting for the sons of God to be revealed, so too the Spirit gathers us up in his own groans for the world, helping us in prayer to carry along the very deepest primordial movements of God in the world. In classic understatement Paul writes, in what must be some of the richest theology in the whole of the New Testament, 'We do not know what we ought to pray for.' Who among us cannot identify with that? However, despite our weakness, or perhaps because of our weakness, 'the Spirit himself intercedes for us with groans that words cannot express.'[41] And lest we think this unmistakably charismatic utterance is something apart from God, something of our own doing, and therefore without effect, we understand that the one who searches our hearts, namely God, 'knows the mind of the Spirit, because the Spirit intercedes for the saints in accordance with God's will.'[42] In short, a groan is enough. A prayer uttered in our weakness, that confirms how inarticulate we are, turns out to be the axis upon which the work of God moves. In agonising, groaning prayer – not polite utterance – God's will is performed.

Which brings us back to where we started: prayer as primary language – honest, gutsy, feisty even. Yes, we need secondary language and we need tertiary language. We need to accomplish things, get things done, communicate what we need, pass on information. All of this is important and necessary. Furthermore, we must not discount the times when it is simply enough in prayer to be silent. Despite what I say earlier about the almost faddish interest in monastic spirituality, contemplative prayer is an important part of our praying tradition and in the present climate of hurriedness has much to commend it. But this is not prayer's dominant note. In prayer, we return to primary language and in the process become our most original. Some of this may carry over, of course, into other forms of speech. It would be my hope that honesty behind closed doors with God will eventuate honesty with others, and, in my own case, honesty in the pulpit. Contained within all this, my hope is that primitive prayer would begin to erode, indeed even scandalise, the daintiness of so much suburban piety. As Forsyth puts it, with reference to the prettiness of suburban piety:

> Our religion may gain some beauty this way, but it loses its vigor. It may gain style, but it loses power. It is good form, but mere aesthetic piety. It may consecrate manners, but it impoverishes the mind. It may regulate prayer by the precepts of intelligence

instead of the needs and faith of the soul. It may feed certain pensive emotions, but it may emasculate will, secularize energy, and empty character. And so we decline to a state of things in which we have no shocking sins – yes, and no splendid souls; when all souls are dully correct, as like as shillings, but as thin, and as cheap.[43]

PART TWO

EMOTIONAL
PRIMITIVISM

Four

In Your Anger Do Not Sin

> Into this complacency Jesus flings his sword, severing the
> very ties that seem to hold life together. He questions every-
> thing that humanly speaking is self-understood, even the
> closest ties of flesh and blood. Once the unrest of Christ has
> been let into a man's heart, he becomes incomprehensible
> and the cause of a scandal.
>
> Romano Guardini, *The Lord*

I count it as a great privilege to have studied at theological seminary. There is simply no substitute for the kind of scholarly
intensity, as well as community, that seminary affords. Even
though I had come from a Bible-believing church, so-called, and
had sat under some great preaching, it was as if I had never read
the Bible before. As with many theological students, through the
experience of college I became thoroughly defamiliarised with
the text I thought I knew, and was plunged instead into the
strange new world of the scriptures.[1]

Every Thursday, however, by way of reminder that our theology must always be rooted in the worshipping life of the church,
the whole of the student body was compelled to attend chapel: to
sing, to pray, to confess sins and to hear preaching. Actually, it
was a welcome break from the routine of going to lectures,
though not a very pleasant experience for the preacher, knowing
full well that over lunch the sermon would be subject to the critical scrutiny of these young, self-possessed theologians.

One of the most memorable sermons I heard at that time was
given by Nigel Lee, who was director at the time of a well-known
missionary organisation. What stands out about that occasion is

that I heard years later that Nigel believed it to be a complete disaster, thus confirming to me yet again that preachers really don't have any idea what is going on in the sermon event. Because the truth is that it was a great sermon. What made it so powerful was the subversive nature of his approach. Here we all were, anticipating a rousing address on the Great Commission, with its inevitable call to go into all the world (it was only a matter of time, we reckoned, before he would make the routine altar call to go to Africa), when the preacher, in a clever outflanking manoeuvre – a bit like Jesus' use of parables – began to talk instead about the subject of anger. It goes without saying that there was hardly a person in the chapel that day for whom anger was not an issue. Furthermore, there was hardly a person present who was not undone by the theme of the sermon. Instead of packing our bags to go off to Africa, we were unpacking our consciences from years of anger.

If ever there is a subject that was designed to prick the conscience of even the godliest Christians it is this one. As a pastor I have had my fair share of angry church members, and I dare say I have vented my own anger, in perhaps more subtle and manipulative ways, on the church (pastors are experts at being passive-aggressive). And in the chapel that day one could sense conviction as Nigel humorously but honestly opened up on his own struggles in this area. But what made the message particularly provocative that morning was his suggestion that not all anger was bad: that anger was as much a virtue in the Christian life as it was a vice. This we had not reckoned on at all. In the tradition I grew up in, which I would describe as mildly puritanical, anger was most definitely one of the seven deadly sins. Just as lust was the forerunner of adultery, so anger, as Jesus said of course, was the precursor to murder, and something to be stamped on whenever its smoke began to surface.[2] 'Do not let the sun go down while you are still angry,' Paul exhorts the Ephesians, 'and do not give the devil a foothold.'[3]

But whilst it is undoubtedly true that anger does not always bring about the righteous life that God desires, there is an equal and opposite danger that in seeking to eradicate anger entirely from our emotional range, we extinguish passion as well; that in our fear of the murderous intent of anger, we end up fearing any semblance of emotional outburst at all. This is particularly true, I think, in the way we bring up children in the Christian community. How much suppressed emotion is there among children who have grown up evangelical, simply because as soon as an extreme emotion like anger began to surface it was sat upon as something entirely negative and definitely not something that had a place within a truly Christian home? My sense is that this is widespread. If the people I have journeyed with over the years are representative of the Christian community at large, then not only are there tremendous advantages in being raised in church, but also terrible consequences, unacknowledged rage being foremost among them. My experience of bringing up my own children confirms to me how easy it is to suppress any kind of anger in our youngsters for fear that it will develop into something uncontrollable. But doing this runs the very real risk of extolling placidity.

Anthony Trollope observes this peculiarly religious kind of emotional repression in the first volume of his *Chronicles of Barsetshire*. The scenario goes something like this: the Archdeacon is fulminating against the assertion that the Hiram's Hospital Funds are not being administered properly. The warden, Mr Harding, received £400 per year and the inmates only 1/8d per day. Mr Harding was deeply hurt about these unjust allegations. But as Trollope notes, rather than giving expression to his hurt, he turned it over in his mind, played his feelings on his cello, and lived his anger quietly, until eventually he emerged with his customary serenity. Trollope's comment about him was that 'he was painfully fearful of having to come to an open quarrel with any person on any subject.'[4]

How many times this kind of repression occurs in the Christian community is anyone's guess. My sense is that psychologists would have a field day in the church, both with congregants and leaders. Presumably one of the reasons for living one's anger quietly in the way that Mr Harding did is an entirely biblical one: namely, that one should be 'quick to listen, slow to speak and slow to become angry, for man's anger does not bring about the righteous life that God desires.'[5] Getting rid of 'all bitterness, rage and anger, brawling and slander, along with every form of malice,' is not only a Christian imperative but, for Paul, one of the hallmarks of authentic life in the Spirit.[6] But again, whilst it is undoubtedly true that forbearance is a virtue, and whilst it is also true that anger often wrecks the possibilities of reconciliation, even so, there is a very real danger that in our attempts to silence our anger we end up silencing our passions; that in our attempts to deal with our lust, we excise our desire; that in our commitment to holiness we end up humourless. And so what I want to do in these next few chapters is to try to explore, if not resolve, the very real conundrum that is present for most believers in knowing what passions we must kill, and what passions, on the other hand, we must perforce allow, lest our piety ends up frigid.

My sense is that we have erred on the side of the former. In other words, our basic evangelical instinct is to crush anything that smacks of the irrational. Whether it is the passion of anger or, to take the other two examples that I want to explore below, the yearning of physical desire or the emotional experience of joy and exuberance, my sense is that there is far too much inhibition masquerading as piety, to the point that it is almost inconceivable for us to imagine an agitated, comical, sensuous person as a holy person. Too quickly, in my opinion, we assume that if something excites our passion then it must, *ipso facto*, be sinful. How many extroverts for example, have we neutered over the years because their exuberance is an embarrassment to our piety? Or how many emotions have we flattened because their violence is a threat to our equilibrium? Our failure to explore a theology of passion has made much of our Christianity an exercise in emotional suppression. If we are to recover a faith that works in the real world and not just in the artificial construct of cultural optimism then it will need to be more familiar with the workings of the heart. We need a Christianity that is conceived as the enlargement of human nature rather than its eradication.

Be ye Angry but do not Sin

Of course, those who have grown up in a house of anger will know that there is almost always a trail of destruction in its wake. There are casualties, not to mention shame and sorrow. For good reason the Bible is generally very negative about this passion. Unchecked anger is itself a distortion of the image of God. And if I am understood to have encouraged by this chapter – and by my advocacy of a more gritty piety in general – a kind of volatile, irresponsible Christian witness, then I will have failed to make my point. For my point is not that we need to be angry in the face of our enemies, but to suggest that sometimes in our desire to curb anger, whether our own or someone else's, we distort the image of God in a different way, conveying through our impassability that the epitome of holiness is the autonomous, detached self. And this we must not do, for passion is what tells us that we are alive. Quell one's passion and one might as well quit living – or at least quit Christianity and become a Buddhist instead. Buddhism, by definition, is about harmony and healing. The Buddha taught that three states of mind are the source of all our unhappiness: ignorance, obsessive desire and anger. Indeed, there is much wisdom in Thich Naht Hahn's classic treatment of the subject: *Anger: Buddhist Wisdom for Cooling the Flames*.[7] Who could not benefit from practising 'mindful breathing' and other such peace-inducing methods, in the way that Hahn advocates? It certainly wouldn't harm. The only problem is: it is not Christianity. Neither Jesus nor Paul would have fared very well under such passivity, and doubtless many subsequent Christian leaders would have struggled also. As the Reformation preacher, Martin Luther, admitted, and as many a writer and preacher will confirm: 'I never work better than when I am inspired by anger; for when I am angry, I can write, pray and preach well, for then my whole temperament is quickened, my understanding sharpened, and all mundane vexations and temperaments depart.'[8] When asked by his wife why, since leaving the pastorate to teach in the seminary, he was not writing anymore, one well-known author replied: 'because I am not angry anymore.' As much as anger can be a very destructive force in one's life, anger also drives our creativity, and oftentimes clarifies our thinking.

In fact, one could go further and say that there are occasions when not only is there nothing wrong with feeling a kind of anger, but that there is everything right. Not to feel anger at the injustice in the world is itself a form of sin – a sign of cowardice as well as culpability. As Bede Jarrett OP says: 'the world needs anger. The world often continues to allow evil, because it does not get angry enough.'[9] Such anger, notes Jonathan Wittenberg – of the kind that is directed against slavery, trafficking in women and children, contempt for refugees and strangers, blindness to the fate of the poor – 'is not the opposite of patience but indifference.'[10] Indeed, given the way the media present these things, saturating us with images of suffering from around the world, it is entirely possible that in modern culture indifference has now taken the place where indignation ought to be.

Whether we can demarcate anger and sin so precisely is a moot point. It is not an exact science. Furthermore, the rendering of Paul's injunction as 'Be ye angry and sin not,' as the *King James Version* has it, is exegetically debatable. For all the merits of this translation and the support it provides to the argument here, my sense is that it probably does not have this take. In all likelihood it simply means what it seems to imply: that in resorting to anger we are on the borderlands of destructive attitudes. Even so, I like the translation, because it suggests that maybe we have a lot further to travel than we have hitherto realised before we get to that border: that it is alright to feel things strongly, and even at times to feel a little agitated. This is not sin, but simply what it means to be human.

No more Mr Nice Guy

Part of the problem is the way we define humility: as if humility was a state of emotional equilibrium. A number of texts come to mind. 'Come to me,' Jesus said, 'all you who are weary and burdened, and I will give you rest. Take my yoke upon you and learn from me, for I am *gentle* and humble in heart, and you will find rest for your souls.'[11] Or, Paul's appeal to the Corinthians by the same 'meekness and *gentleness* of Christ'.[12] 'As apostles of Christ,' he says to the Christians at Thessalonica, 'we were *gentle* among you, like a mother caring for her little children.'[13] And thus it is that we imagine Jesus and Paul as the very epitome of mildness and discretion, and ourselves as humble underlings who, as soon as the passions flare, are acting out of less than righteous motives.

Yet, even a cursory reading of the gospels and the epistles will tell us that this is not the whole picture. Humility cannot possibly mean docility any more than gentleness can mean passionlessness, for the Jesus who invites us into his *gentle* heart is the same Jesus who, indignant with the money changers in the temple, makes a whip out of cords and drives them away.[14] To those who think it impious to feel exasperated or frustrated, the gospels reveal to us, in their presentation of Jesus' response to the disciples' lack of faith, that anger is very much part of an authentic spiritual life. As Mark Galli points out, we present a Jesus 'meek and mild', since that is what our tradition bequeaths to us, when in fact the gospel presents to us a Jesus 'mean and wild': a Jesus who pours scorn on the Pharisees; treats Herod with derision; speaks sternly to the leper; turns over tables in the temple.[15] Likewise, the Paul who appeals to the Corinthians by the 'meekness and *gentleness* of Christ' is the same Paul who threatens to come in power and not in weakness, should the Corinthians not repent of their defection over to those who masquerade as servants of Christ.[16]

What this means for those who are responsible for the spiritual formation of Christian communities is that we must think again about how we imagine a gentle person to be. Is a gentle person a soft touch; someone who we can take for a ride? Or is it that a gentle person is known as gentle precisely because we find in that person the coming together of strength and grace? Increasingly, I have come to believe the latter. As it turns out, a gentle person is not a spineless person. On the contrary. To be gentle is to be full of conviction. And this virtue is forged, more often than not, in the fire of conflict rather than the place of comfort.

In a sermon entitled 'No More Reverend Nice Guy', preached at Durham Cathedral, Stephen Cherry explores this theme of spiritual toughness. Noting the very common tendency among Christian leaders to neuter their passion for the sake of virtue, Cherry demurs, noting that 'it is very possible to be both gentle and firm, gentle and honest, gentle and effective.' There is nothing sentimental, he argues, about being gentle. Gentleness is the preserve not of the timid but the brave. They are gentle, precisely because they are honest. In *Barefoot Disciple*, which came out a couple of years later, Cherry makes a similar point, referring to Palm Sunday:

Maybe the point of Palm Sunday is to help us to understand that humility and self-presentation, not to mention humility and passion, can indeed be deeply and profoundly connected . . . This sort of humility is assertive and bold. It is energising and empowering. It is all of a piece with the courage and vulnerability that is revealed on the donkey, in the Temple and ultimately on the cross.[17]

Given the extremity of Jesus' righteous indignation, and its central place within the passion narratives, it seems inconceivable that a meek and mild Jesus was allowed to prevail. Far from presenting a one-dimensional Jesus, the gospels bear witness to an astonishing emotional range.

Whether our communities can stomach such forthrightness, such willingness to confront the real issues, is far from certain. The spirituality of niceness is well-nigh ubiquitous. But if, as Cherry notes, we are serious about the virtuous life then we will have to reconsider this state of affairs, because 'these practices,' says Cherry, 'these habits, these virtues, do not of themselves lead to the saccharine spider's web of niceness in which far too many Christians – especially ordained ones – have been or are trapped. Rather, they are robust, earthy, strong, humane virtues the practice of which renders us as potent but as vulnerable as Christ.' Indeed, the practice of niceness, he observes, 'is actually a form of both avoidance and self defence.'[18]

The same is true with the issue of forgiveness. In the Christian community there has long been a misconception that forgiveness means the absence of hurt or anger on the part of the one injured: a kind of celestial forgetfulness that is quickly able to sweep an injustice under the carpet, all in the name of love. After all, we are Christians are we not, and isn't being a Christian by definition to forgive? Didn't Jesus himself say something about forgiving others their sins, in order that we too might be forgiven our sins? Indeed he did.[19] And ever since, the willingness to offer forgiveness has been right at the core of what it means to be truly Christian. As John Wesley apparently said to a man who vowed he could never forgive: 'Then, sir, I hope you never sin.'

But just because this imperative stands over us does not mean we can easily avoid some level of emotional turmoil. To truly forgive, one must first of all register the very real injury that has been done. Otherwise, all that the forgiveness will represent is simply our attempt to keep the peace; and the speed with which we seek to offer forgiveness will reveal nothing more than our fear of pain rather than our depth of piety. As my friend Simon Walsh reminded me, from his own experience of working on the peace process in Colombia, it is not just reconciliation we are after, but truth and reconciliation. And truth implies anger before there will ever be healing.

Again, there is good reason why we have this state of affairs. Often the reason why we seek to forgive so quickly, too quickly in some instances, is because we know the dangers of not so doing. I have hesitated to write this chapter, because like most church leaders, I have witnessed firsthand the destruction caused by bitterness and unforgiveness. As William Blake's poem *A Poison Tree* testifies:

> I was angry with my friend:
> I told my wrath, my wrath did end.
> I was angry with my foe:
> I told it not, my wrath did grow . . .[20]

And such is the power of bitterness that it can take on a corporate dimension as well as an individual. The writer to the Hebrews is right to warn the church of a root of bitterness, because if it is allowed to grow it will inevitably defile many.[21] But that said, what we must not countenance in reaction is spiritual passivity, because for all its appearance of godliness, quietism actually neuters the soul. Christian holiness is not resigned passivity; it is vigorous humility. And unless we recover this kind of piety for the church, my sense is that the church will continue to appeal to certain personality types, but ostracise others.

Where the line is between passionate humility and rudeness is a moot point. Some of the more recent attacks on suburban nice-ness, including this one I dare say, need to be careful not to con-fuse earthiness with downright crudity. A vicar once made a virtue of his expletives in the pulpit, and whilst he could cite a number of texts which seemed to justify his behaviour, my own conviction is that he had gone too far. In seeking to redress what is perceived as the feminisation of the church we need to be careful that an equally stereotypical masculine image of the church does not prevail in its place – a piety that amounts to nothing more than lads drinking lager, watching footie, and learning not to cry. Not only would such a move be retrograde, it would not even be true to the very best traditions of muscular Christianity which was not so much about proving that one was a lad, but more about proving that one was a man.

But that aside, what we must not permit any longer in our sub-urban setting is a pious daintiness that skirts round the real issues of life. If ever there was a time, culturally, for Christianity to offer a robust, humane, and intense piety, it is now. The senti-mentalisation of culture – British culture in particular – has been happening for a while now. Apparently, we have been 'faking it' in all kinds of areas of life, including religion, often by quelling our most violent emotions.[22] And even if it remains a cardinal Christian virtue to subsume one's anger for the sake of peace, or to suffer long with those who irritate us, let us remember that an important part of holy living is also to have the courage, at cer-tain times, to speak the truth in love, not simply in our personal relationships but also, as we noted in a previous chapter, in our relationship with God. As Kathleen O'Connor remarks concern-ing the protest language that appears in the book of Lament-ations: 'It prevents us from sliding prematurely over suffering towards happy endings.' Raised as she was in a loving family, but one that forbade anger and ignored sorrow, 'some of us lost great chunks of ourselves in the process.'[23] But what Lamentations gave back to her in her relationship to God, quite apart from her relationships with others, was the piety of anger. As Lytta Basset similarly notes, 'To rebel against God does not seem at first glance to be a life choice. Religious education has a lot to do with this, given its propensity to confuse submission to authorities and submission to God. The biblical God, however, is always in search of a human face, be it smiling or frowning in anger.'[24]

In the following chapters I want to extend this discussion about the human emotion to other evangelical taboos such as physical desire and even humour, because much of our piety in the suburbs tends towards the ancient heresy of docetism. Docetism comes from the Greek word *dokeo*: to seem. It contends that Jesus was not fully human but rather only seemed to be human. Not surprisingly, indeed most significantly, docetism circumvents the scandal of the cross by claiming that the real Christ departed just prior to the crucifixion. All told, docetism translates into a Jesus who wafts about three inches about the ground, making wise, pithy pronouncements about life as he gazes into the blue yonder of the Galilean hills (indeed, if one reads carefully the plethora of books in recent years which are searching for the historical Jesus, this is precisely the image we are left with). Applied to Christian spirituality, this weak, spiritually frigid image translates into a peculiarly disembodied piety amongst the faithful: an overly spiritual piety that plays into the hands of all the worst aspects of suburban blandness.

What I hope to show in the following chapters is that a piety worthy of the name Christian will need to be far more concrete. Since the gospels present a fully alive, fully human Jesus, who laughed and wept and raged and loved, so our piety must reflect this also – a piety that is as human as it is holy; as sensual as it is serious; and as emotional as it is earnest. Anything less than this will consign our suburban piety to that peculiarly Protestant tendency towards Gnosticism, and the call of Christ in a person's life as something desperately conformist rather than the radical transformation that it really is.

Five

Delighting in Our Desires

I remember the thought I used then to have of holiness . . . It
appeared to me that there was nothing in it but what was
ravishingly lovely.

Jonathan Edwards, *The Way of Holiness*

For the lack of desire is the ill of all ills;
Many thousands through it the dark pathway have trod;
The balsam, the wine of predestinate wills,
Is a jubilant pining and longing for God.

Frederick Faber, *Desire of God*

I am a nonconformist and proud of it. The stringency of our tradition in terms of plain worship and unadorned buildings has
something very prophetic about it. Not without justification,
we keep our churches simple, in order that our focus might be
upon God and not upon created beauty. And for the most part
it seems to work. But at other times, if we are honest, it can
really get to you. We long for something more sensual.
Compared to the sumptuousness of our high-church brethren,
our spiritual diet can seem very meagre indeed. The funniest
take I have read on this is by Garrison Keillor in *Lake Wobegon*
– that fictitious Midwest town in America, full of second- and
third-generation Norwegian Lutherans and Exclusive
Brethren, as Keillor himself once used to be. It all comes to a
head one Christmas. Sitting in the living room of his Aunt Flo's
house, singing plain songs with ever so plain voices, he can
hear the Catholics whooping it up next door in the high Mass,
and longs to be there.[1]

I have a lot of sympathy with this. My own Christian formation took place in the context of low-church puritanism, not high-
church Roman Catholicism, and even though the puritanism was
more than compensated for by a powerful and charismatic
dimension, strangely it was the conservativism that prevailed, to
the point that we made a virtue of the ability to not conform.
Piety was a matter of what you said no to, rather than what you
could say yes to. Like most puritans we had this terrible fear that
somewhere, somehow, someone was enjoying themselves.

The asceticism that puritans are renowned for is a travesty of
what is actually the case. For positive views about sex, and some
of the most erotic love poetry of the seventeenth century, the
puritans cannot be bettered.[2] But sadly little of this permeated
down. Within a few centuries evangelicalism became synonymous with a world-denying asceticism.

The hermeneutic of suspicion that characterises the puritan
conscience is not an entirely bad one, of course. I hope I never
lose that suspicion, for it reflects something of the Bible's own
suspicion about the motives, deceitfulness even, of the human
heart. Jeremiah got it right: 'The heart is deceitful above all
things.'[3] Moreover, it may well be that a rediscovery of this pious
introspection is just what is needed in the present climate where
grace is operating in some quarters as nothing more than an easy
option – cheap grace, as Bonhoeffer would call it, demanding
very little by way of repentance. Maybe so. Nevertheless, whilst
puritanical sensibility is an important strand of Christian piety,
an overdeveloped asceticism is death to the church, and death to
Christian formation in general, because it effectively calls into
question all creative impulses as inherently sinful, strangling
them at birth. No matter that David danced with all his might
before the Lord; no matter that the Bible contains some of the
most erotic poetry in all of literature; no matter that many stories
in the gospels are scented with the smells of perfume and spices.
The fact of the matter is that when a recent book on great figures
in revival came to describe the virtues of Duncan Campbell, possibly one of the greatest revivalists, it simply stated: 'It wasn't just
that Duncan Campbell was a non-smoker, a total abstainer and
hated dancing, his whole desire was to be surrendered to God in
the very manner of his daily life.'[4] From which statement we are

to conclude, apparently, that godliness in a man will mean the cancellation of life for the sake of the upward calling of Christ.

The oddness of the situation is that Jesus was accused of the exact opposite: not of asceticism but of excess. If we want to think ascetic, we need to go to John the Baptist; Jesus, on the other hand, was the party goer – 'a glutton and a drunkard' so they said.[5] He wasn't guilty of either of these sins of course – nor did he smoke for that matter – but he must have done something to have deserved that description, something that set himself in clear contrast to the world-denying piety of the renewalists of his day. Indeed, when we observe closely the life and ministry of Jesus there is a very real sense in which he fits the later rabbinical tradition which argues that the judgement of God will be determined not by how many pleasures we denied ourselves, but on how many we refused. In which case, we must admit that the Christian imagination is hugely under-developed. It has this miraculous ability to turn wine into water, reduce mountains into molehills.

A Poet of Wonder

Perhaps the best illustration of this ambiguity inherent in our desires is the Jesuit poet Gerard Manley Hopkins. Of all the poets Hopkins is the one I go back to. I carry a copy of his poems in my bag, and often will go to sleep with the words of some Hopkins poem in my mind. I think it is something about the Welsh rhythm and lyrical cadences that comforts my soul and helps me to believe.[6] What is staggering about Hopkins, however, and lamentable as regards the history of literature, is that most of Hopkins' early poems have been lost to us. As his biographer points out, Hopkins burnt all his earliest poems in the conviction that poetry in praise of the creation was not fitting for one dedicated to following Christ. As a rigorous Jesuit he just couldn't bring himself to believe that God could in any way be pleased with his sensuality and his love of beauty.[7] In fact, it was only by stumbling upon the works of Duns Scotus, the medieval Franciscan scholar from whom he acquired his notion of inscape, that finally his soul was set free – 'sways my spirits to peace,' to use Hopkins' own words

– to celebrate in his poetry the prodigious nature of the created world. The poem *God's Grandeur*, which begins with the sumptuous lines: 'The world is charged with the grandeur of God/It will flame out, like shining from shook foil/It gathers to a greatness like the ooze of oil/Crushed,'[8] could only come from the pen of someone who had finally been reconciled to the sensuality of God's created world, in the way that Scotus encouraged.

What interests me about Hopkins is that his struggle with poetry is illustrative of the very real tensions that exist, for all Christians it seems to me, between the call to self-denial and the energy of their creativity – with many Christians concluding, sadly, that since the creative side of their spirituality sounds for all the world like self-actualisation, it therefore must be sinful. How many actors, or how many dancers, for instance, have given up their vocation because it doesn't seem congruent with the call to deny oneself and take up one's cross? Or how many Christians, generally, leave vast tracts of their emotional life unexplored out of fear of what it might unleash? The experience of Andrew Krivak, as he makes his way through the various stages of the Jesuit novitiate, is testimony to the draconian, almost inhumane, destruction of the creative impulse within certain traditions of the Christian faith. Little wonder that he was unable to complete the course. The ascetic way he embraced was so hostile to the poet that was inside him that had he stayed he would have denied not simply the sin that 'crouches at the door' but also the very essence of who God had created him to be.[9]

Clearly, there is a very real sense in which, as followers of Christ, we must crucify the flesh. Of that there is no doubt. Cruciformity is the very essence of Christian discipleship. But the fundamental question is: to what does *flesh* refer? If it refers to human desire gone wrong then, by all means, we must crucify these things because they are inimical to the life of faith. Indeed, this is precisely what life according to *sarx* encompasses: a life lived contrary to the classical virtues of love, humility and kindness.[10] But if by flesh we mean the putting to death of all human desire and longing, which too often, sadly, is how *flesh* is interpreted, then what happens in its wake is the destruction not simply of sin but sensuality as well; the eradication not simply of idols, but art. By making *flesh* synonymous with physicality, we destroy not just the bad bits but the good bits. In fact, by defining *flesh* in terms of the rejection of the simple ordinary gestures of our humanity, then what we are left with by way of spirituality is not technically Christian but Gnostic because, as Oliver O'Donovan points out, resurrection means the reaffirmation of our humanity not its denial.[11] Christianity is the way of incarnation; the affirmation of human relatedness; the redemption of physicality. The redemption that comes through Jesus Christ relates to a salvation *of* the world, not a salvation *from* the world.

Mountains or Deserts?

Having asserted the importance of a healthy doctrine of creation, alongside a more typical and instinctive doctrine of redemption, even I have to say that God does not seem to play fair. For the God who awakens within us a sense of beauty is the same one who expects us to temper this with restraint. The call to take up the cross remains *the* distinctive call upon the life of the Christian, not just against those obvious sins in our lives but even those good things. And at times this seems almost impossible to do. The power of beauty, of art, of a person, can be so overwhelming, so life giving, so energising, that to take up one's cross and deny oneself seems a radical denial of the very things that God inhabits.[12]

Sara Maitland has an interesting take on this in her exploration of silence and solitude. Appealing to a kind of spiritual geography, she describes these two impulses in our tradition – self-denying and world affirming – as akin to the retreat to the desert on the one hand or the escape to the mountains on the other. That is, she sees the desert as the place where silence strips away our false ego, and the mountain where, in contrast, the individual finds itself and gives voice to its passions in a great swathe of romantic feeling.[13] She writes about these things with some authority since she lives most of her life as a hermit.

But whilst Maitland is helpful in describing two major spiritual and literary traditions, in no way does this resolve the conundrum. For instance, what do you do if you have both of these impulses coursing through your veins at the same time: the self-denial of the cross versus the desire of the soul for beauty? What then? Even Sara Maitland is forced to choose, and in the end forsakes the solitude of the desert for the wildness of the mountains. She is a romantic, after all. But what if you are committed to both: committed to the way of the cross, and yet, at the same time, alert to the sensuality of creation? What then?

There is no easy way out of this one. To be a Christian is to be tethered to a doctrine of creation as well as a doctrine of redemption: a conviction that even though our humanity is marred, nevertheless it is one that has been fashioned in the image of God. We must not too quickly deny ourselves the pleasures of our created world, lest we also starve the soul of its basic nutrients. So, it seems to me that some risks need to be taken here. This is not an exact science. There are times, to be sure, when in pursuit of a creative impulse, we may well step over the mark. There may even be times when, in pursuit of a vocational pull, we may seem to be acting selfishly. Take working mothers. Is this not one of the charges made against working mothers: that if they were truly Christian they would forsake their career, and return to the home? But as Bonnie J. Miller-McLemore points out, it may well be that all that is happening here is the result of wrong notions of self-denial, tantamount to self-destruction, rather than selfishness on the part of the woman.[14]

Or maybe it is the case that God wants us to die to these things, simply because he wants us to receive them back, only this time purified of its potential idolatry. After all, as Calvin once said, the human heart is an idol factory. Even the most innocent of pleasures has the power to seduce our hearts. There is a fine line between enjoyment of a thing and dependency on it; a fine line between gratitude and addiction. Thus, in order for these things to continue, some kind of regular detachment needs to occur, if only to prove to ourselves that we really are free. Perhaps we see this most clearly in human friendship, where two souls can become so absorbed into one another, so entwined, that in order to avoid the suffocation of idolatrous love a kind of dying needs to take place; or maybe, to take another example, a creative talent, where the need to perform becomes so important, so essential to one's existence, that a certain relinquishment needs to occur, lest one's identity becomes entirely bound up with one's gift. As Paul Borgman observes in his commentary on the patriarchal narratives in Genesis: all blessing involves relinquishment.[15] In order to realise the promise of land, Abraham must leave his country and his people. Likewise, in order to perpetuate the promise at the end of the story, Abraham must be willing to sacrifice his beloved son, Isaac, however outrageous it may seem; otherwise there is every chance that the gift, Isaac, will end up more important than the Giver.

That the Lord stops Abraham in his tracks and prevents him from slaying his son assures us that faith is on the side of life. God is not a sadist, nor does he make a virtue out of self-abnegation *per se*. Those who end up flagellating themselves, be they monks or lay people, are not at the top end of Christian spirituality, but rather at the bottom, violating the grace of the gospel with an introspection that is less than healthy. But conversely, those who refuse to relinquish anything in this life, for fear of abandonment, violate the gospel that Abraham announced, because the essence of it is to trust God, placing him above all other human loves.

Sex and Spirituality

This painful and often misunderstood tension between denial and desire, between the ascetic and the aesthete, comes to a head most acutely in the area of sex and sexuality and for the most part the ascetic has prevailed. Indeed, the subject of sex has proven to be a great embarrassment to the church: note the interpretative issues, as well as hilarity, surrounding the Song of Songs as exegetes try to circumvent the overt eroticism of the book by way of spiritualised allegory. Having worked my way through the Song one autumn with the evening congregation at Millmead, I will never be able to look at a christening in the same way ever again, for in their eagerness to bypass the clear and unambiguous meaning of the text, the ancients interpret the navel that is referred to in chapter seven, which to all the world refers to a woman's midriff, possibly even as the secret place of the woman's vulva, as the baptismal font and the efficacious sacrament![16]

Part of our problem is that very early on the church reworked the very earthy, physicality of Hebrew spirituality into Greek

Platonism, thus rendering the body and the soul not merely different but opposed to one another. In other words, the more spiritual one became the less physical one had to be. For instance when Margery Kempe had a vision from God, the first thing she did was to announce to her husband that she would no longer be having sex with him.[17] This is not an isolated incident. There is a whole tradition, going back to the very earliest days of the church whereby some have become eunuchs for the sake of the kingdom.

This is all very well. Maybe we have made too much of sex, and refused to explore the possibilities of a life of chastity.[18] Furthermore, maybe some of our more recent Christian expressions of sexual freedom are nothing more than a trivialisation of sex. There is a very real danger that the present reaction in the church to Victorian stuffiness on the subject of sex is actually fostering in its stead crude innuendos, with the Song of Songs, for example, reduced to nothing more than a sex manual. But if innuendo is one thing, and something to be avoided when coming to the text, allegory is quite another problem and an error of equal magnitude. By allegorising the eroticism of the love between a man and a woman, by diverting this passion into a spiritualised form, we render spiritual love, or what we refer to as agape love, as something less than physical, less than passionate, and less than sensual. By taking the desire out of spiritual love the church becomes a very cold place indeed.

Such a scenario is unnecessary as well as tragic, for whatever else the Song of Songs is – and at the very least it is a highly erotic love poem – it is also, by way of analogy, a celebration of the highly charged, often tempestuous relationship between Christ and the church. The reason the Song of Songs snuck into the canon of scripture is not simply to celebrate the sexual love of a man and a woman, although it does that *par excellence*, but also because there is something intensely sensual and physical about our relationship to God. Coming to faith in Christ is not the death of passion but its beginning. As C.S. Lewis states, casting his eye back no doubt on the Presbyterian austerity of his youth, but also with reference to the philosophical influence of Stoicism on Christian faith: 'It would seem that Our Lord finds our desires not too strong but too weak.'[19] Not without significance does Paul, when he wants to describe his longing for union with Christ, use a word that in Greek denotes sexual union between a man and a woman. Alan Ecclestone provocatively but wisely notes, 'The primitive impulse to deify sexual love was not wholly misguided; it has all the features of great mystical experience, abandon, ecstasy, polarity, dying, rebirth and perfect union . . . It prompts between human beings those features characteristic of prayer; a noticing, a paying attention, a form of address, a yearning to communicate at ever deeper levels of being, an attempt to reach certain communion with the other.'[20]

Indeed, there are times in the Psalms, as Robert Alter points out, when the longing for the presence of God borders on the erotic. The Hebrew word *yedidot*, he argues, which occurs at the beginning of Psalm 84, 'is associated with *dod*, "lover," and *dodim*, "lovemaking," and conveys a virtually erotic intensity in the speakers' longing for the temple on Mount Zion,'[21] and hence should be translated 'lovely' as opposed to the rather tame 'amiable' of the *King James Version*: 'How amiable are thy tabernacles, O LORD of hosts.'

In short, if erotic love needs to be sanctified in order to protect it from lust, so agape love needs to be eroticised in order to protect it from law. Agape love and eros love are not different kinds of love, any more than philos love and agape love. On this point I must disagree with Lewis.[22] Exegetically they are interchangeable, and emotionally they are cousins. The difference is in degree rather than in kind. Agape love and eros love play themselves out on a continuum, rather than on separate and parallel lines. In fact, rather than seeing agape love as the ultimate expression of eros love, how about seeing eros love as the ultimate expression of agape love?[23] When – as a secular rationalist – Etty Hillesum found herself in the embarrassing position of wanting to kneel down to pray, she discovered that there is something incredibly intimate about this moment, something undeniably erotic about this bodily gesture before God. As Patrick Woodhouse notes, 'For Etty, this is no cold act of piety. "Such things," she writes, "are often more intimate even than sex."'[24] Bernard of Clairvaux, who was never one to mince his words when it came to passion for Christ, takes the first line of the Song as an invitation to a level of desire that would shock even the most tactile of congregations. Reflecting on the spiritual longings of the woman at the feet of Jesus, and the sensuality of the eucharist, Bernard notes:

> 'I cannot be at peace,' she says, 'until he kisses me with the kisses of his mouth. I give thanks for the kiss of his feet, and for the kiss of his hand; but if he cares for me at all, let him kiss me with the kisses of his mouth. I am not ungrateful, but I love. I have received more than I deserve . . . but less than I want. Desire moves me, not reason. Modesty indeed protests, but love conquers.'[25]

If this language is legitimate, and consistent with the best traditions of the Bible, the church makes a big mistake when it castigates the world for its sensuality. It makes a mistake, not in trying to maintain a moral position, but because in a culture in which sexual orgasm is one of the few places that one can experience real transcendence, a gospel of sin management seems a poor alternative. The result is deadly: a form of holiness that looks strangely reminiscent of middle-class conformity, and not the passionate life for which Christ died. Not only is this kind of gospel unattractive, it cannot ultimately redeem, for as John Donne laments in the fourteenth of the holy sonnets, 'for I, Except you enthral me, never shall be free, Nor ever chaste, except you ravish me.'[26] In other words, his lesser love can only be overcome by a divine seduction. Tempting as it was for Donne to leave behind his sensual past, and portray religious piety as something other than this, Donne understood that religious love and sensual love were two sides of the same coin.[27] Rather than abandoning his passions when he came to Christian faith, Donne understood that those passions needed to be harnessed for an even greater seduction by the one true God; and that only this could liberate us from our worst self.

Strangely enough it was the puritans who explored this aspect of spirituality in their notion of 'the expulsive power of a higher affection'. It sounds painful, but what they meant by this phrase was the need for the soul to be ravished by love if it was ever to have a chance of overcoming sin. Sin management, as it is practiced in the churches, is not enough; we need a new affection, and of a kind that does not send us into flights of fancy, but roots us in the very stuff of our humanity. For unless we cultivate a spirituality that takes seriously the passions of the human heart, not only will we have succumbed to the church's oldest adversary, namely Gnosticism, but we will also have offered to the world a parody of the real thing, because, of course, the goal of sanctification is not to make us more spiritual, but to make us more human.

In the final chapter of part two I want to explore the implications of that final statement as it relates to humour and laughter. Given the propensity to define spirituality as something less than human, then my sense, and indeed my experience, is that humour is regarded as something less than pious. But if we are defining spiritual piety as an exercise in restoring our full humanity – if, as Irenaeus once remarked, 'the glory of God is a man full alive' – then maybe we have got this wrong. Maybe laughter is at the very heart of a saintly life in just the same way sensuality is.

Six

Surprised by Joy

Either we dismiss the Good News as too good to be true, or we permit ourselves to be overwhelmingly joyful persons because of it.

Brennan Manning, *The Signature of Jesus*

Umberto Eco is one of the most celebrated intellectuals of our day. He came to public attention with his novel *The Name of the Rose*.[1] Unfortunately, having watched it as a film before reading it as a novel, I cannot imagine William Baskerville as anyone other than James Bond in a monk's garb, since the part is played by Sean Connery. But be that as it may, Eco's bestselling novel tells the story of a Dominican community in the Italian mountains where a series of murders take place. Baskerville, a Franciscan sleuth, is called in to investigate and eventually traces the crimes to the old, blind librarian Jorge, who exercises a pathological hatred of anyone who so much as gets near a certain book: namely, the second book of the *Poetics* of Aristotle, in which the great philosopher writes about the virtues of laughter. So great is Jorge's fear that the students will read this book that he laces the book with poisonous ink.

It seems an odd book to want to forbid. One could understand a monastery wanting to ban some medieval equivalent of *Lady Chatterley's Lover*, say, or the latest Jackie Collins, but to ban a book about laughter seems preposterous. Laughter is what makes us human. But Jorge's fear – and on this he represents the fear of the church as a whole – is that to permit laughter is to allow victory to the devil. Laughter for the old monk represents 'weakness, corruption, the foolishness of our flesh. It is the peasant's entertainment, the drunkard's licence.'[2] To permit laughter, or rather for the monks to know that the great philosopher Aristotle encouraged laughter, would mean that the people of God 'would be transformed into an assembly of monsters belched forth from the abysses of the *terra incognita*, and at that moment the edge of the known world would become the heart of the Christian empire, the Arimaspi on the throne of Peter, Blemmyes in the heart of the monastery, dwarfs with huge bellies and immense heads in charge of the library.'[3]

Well, if old Jorge was fearful that the church in subsequent generations would break out in mirth, he needn't have been. The church, throughout history, has hardly been noted for its jollity. Quite the opposite. As Robert Louis Stevenson noted in his journal: 'I went to church today and am not depressed,' presumably because his usual experience was to come away feeling utterly bleak.[4] I read somewhere, though I cannot find the source, that there was a certain man who was so morose that the last thing he did before going to church was to take the perch out of the budgie's case. I guess he felt that if he wasn't going to have fun on the Lord's Day then neither was his pet budgie. Indeed, certain Christian traditions seem to make a virtue of their dourness. Not only is laugher forbidden, but sombreness is positively encouraged. I heard recently of a denomination in the States who make it a rule never to smile, since to smile is to concede to the sins of the flesh. It reminds me of what Ellen Glasgow wrote about her Presbyterian Father: 'He was entirely unselfish, and in his long life he never committed a pleasure.'[5]

The reason I focus on laughter in the context of primitive piety is because it strikes me that piety in suburbia is a decidedly – and increasingly – serious affair. A bit like the way that modern sportsmen have forgotten how to smile, it seems that we also have lost our ability to enjoy ourselves. Entertainment is one thing; suburbanites are very good at this. But in terms of our capacity to embrace life in all its wonder, to experience joy at the simple things, it appears that the world of statistics has burdened even our leisure time with the need to perform. We do leisure, but do not know how to be leisurely. We are entertained, but seldom experience real mirth. In our disenchanted world of management and assessment we have lost the joy of the amateur: namely, the person who does something for the sheer pleasure of doing it. Think of how sport has mutated in the last few decades into big business; or think of the way music is now mediated via contractual relations. In short, our Protestant work ethic has permeated almost every aspect of our lives, including our churches, so that even Sunday worship becomes an exercise, if we are not careful, in getting something out of it, rather than simply celebrating the mysteries of the faith. In fact, this is so much a part of us now that we are hardly aware that we are doing it. A pastor friend of mine once said to me that when he looks out on the congregation on a Sunday morning, he is sometimes reminded of what St Theresa of Avila once said: 'from silly devotions and sour-faced saints, save us O Lord.' As one Ghanaian Christian pointed out to me recently, with genuine bewilderment: 'You sing songs about dancing, but no one dances.' We say we rejoice in the Lord, but convey by our worship that this joy is so deep down in my heart that the chances of it surfacing on our faces is as remote as an Elvis sighting.

Did Jesus Laugh?

Those who take this sombre line in things spiritual argue that they have the Bible on their side. With John Chrysostom as the best-known proponent, they argue that the gospels never record that Jesus laughed. In one sense this is true. Not once does the Bible say that Jesus broke down in tears of laughter, or that he chuckled in response to some witticism on the part of one of the disciples. But then again, neither does it record that he went to the toilet; and unless we are going to suggest that Jesus was one stop short of a full humanity (which one suspects is what many Christians actually believe, and where the root of the problem lies)[6] then we can assume that not only did he possess all the normal bodily functions associated with the digestive system, but that he also abandoned himself at times to something approaching raucous laughter. Somewhere in those biting ironies and parabolic twists, he must at least have permitted himself a wry smile.

In fact, I imagine Jesus as gloriously free, and unashamedly himself. Laughter for him was not something less than holy. It

did not sit uncomfortably with his quietness. For Jesus to laugh
did not require some contortion of his otherwise mild-mannered
piety. Rather it was just another one of those gestures that
becomes possible in a man fully alive to God – in Jesus' case,
supremely alive. What I mean is, we do not need to suspend holy
living in order to indulge in a bit of humour; nor must we feel
ashamed. On the contrary, the pleasures of irony, jesting, teasing,
and the like, are precisely what we might expect among holy people. That Desmond Tutu, possibly one of the most important
Christian leaders of our generation, should also be a man given
to much laughter and smiling should not surprise us in the least,
but instead seem entirely natural. Jesus may have been a man of
sorrows, but he was also a friend of sinners, and I defy anyone to
deny that there was not at least some merry-making around the
table where he sat.

If a man cannot laugh then he cannot cry. Or to put it the more
usual way: if a man cannot cry then he cannot laugh. In other
words, they are not mutually exclusive emotions, but flip sides of
the same coin. And as much as we want the permission to cry, we
also must give ourselves permission not to take ourselves so seriously so that we can laugh as well. Spurgeon, the renowned
Baptist preacher, is often represented as a dour figure but, as
Peter Morden points out, the truth was that he loved laughter.
Spurgeon once commented that some Christians seemed to have
invented an extra commandment, 'Thou shalt pull a long face on
a Sunday.' In fact, as Morden notes, '[Spurgeon's] own attitude
was somewhat different! "I would rather hear people laugh," he
said, "than I would see them asleep in the house of God."
Humour and happiness could be just as "holy" as tears, he rea-
soned. Moreover laughter could open a door for a person to hear
and receive God's message.'[7]

Anyone familiar with the Rule of Benedict, perhaps one of the
most important pieces of spiritual writing in the whole of
Christendom, will know that this unashamedness about laughter
does not reconcile too easily with what Benedict had to say about
the matter. In fact, I have it on good authority that it is one of the
problems that many Benedictine monks themselves have with
the Rule. Whereas in many other respects the Rule evinces a thoroughly humane and warm spirituality, on the point of laughter it

is quite prickly. In chapter seven of the Rule, in a sustained discussion of what constitutes humility, Benedict warns against much speaking, for 'in much speaking there is no escape from sin.' Concerning the tenth degree of humility however, Benedict counsels that a monk 'be not ready and quick to laugh, for it is written, "The fool lifts up his voice in laughter."' He goes on, saying that when a monk speaks 'he do so gently and without laughter, humbly and seriously, in few and sensible words, and that he be not noisy in speech.'[8]

Speaking with a Benedictine monk from a nearby community, he admitted to being somewhat puzzled himself by this aspect of the Rule, because wherever there is community, he admitted, one will always find humour. So we guess, although we cannot be sure, that what Benedict was against was not laughter as such, but crudity or frivolity. In fact, although Benedict does not demonstrate his awareness of this, there is within the Bible not only a relationship between laughter and unbelief – Sarah being the most notable example[9] – but also a condemnation of the kind of laughter that is found among the rich of this world: what we might call a self-satisfied laughter that will one day be overturned according to Jesus by weeping and wailing. Luke's version of the Beatitudes backs up the 'Blessed are you who weep now, for you will laugh'[10] with a 'Woe to you who laugh now, for you will mourn and weep.'[11] James, his half-brother, urges the rich of Jerusalem to 'Grieve, mourn and wail' and to 'Change your laughter to mourning and your joy to gloom.'[12]

These warnings are very much part of our tradition and a necessary rejoinder to a culture that 'amuses itself to death'. I feel myself that one of the missing ingredients in so much of what we do in the church is a real sense of gravitas. But to interpret these warnings as a blanket condemnation of laughing seems to be stretching the point too far. Laughter is one of those 'signals of transcendence' that sociologist Peter Berger writes about: one of those ordinary human gestures that gives rumour of angels.[13] Some of the most humorous people I know are those who have found themselves as spiritual leaders of their communities. It is as if humour and holiness are bedfellows.

Question: why is it that angels fly? Answer: because they take themselves lightly. Humour reminds us, perhaps like nothing else, that we are not that important after all; that there is something wonderfully unnecessary about the world we live in.[14] Here we are in our consumer world of statistics and economics, busting a gut in order to achieve, taking ourselves oh so seriously, but the holy fool comes along to remind us that we are not indispensable.

The Kingdom of God is a Party

Again, at the risk of over-qualifying, it is important to say what this is not. This is not a treatise for a eupeptic kind of Christianity. Having argued for a need of the church to embrace the wintry seasons of its life, it would be an odd thing indeed to overturn this for the sake of back-slapping, party-going cheerfulness. The fact of the matter is, as Ecclesiastes reminds us, 'there is a time to weep and a time to laugh,'[15] and no amount of *positivity* on the part of the church, to use a word that has become common parlance these days, should prevent us from the inalienable human right of being sad.

All we are simply saying is that when it is a time to laugh – and there will be plenty of those – we should do it wholeheartedly. The joy of the Lord is not simply a pious phrase but an actual feeling. When we laugh we should not imagine ourselves less than holy, but rather as those who are free to give vent to the whole range of emotions possible for those who are made in the image of God. God laughs; and so must we. We must laugh the laughter of the redeemed. Not without significance, certain traditions within the Christian church insist on laughter on Easter Sunday – *risu paschalis* – because the resurrection is God's laugh on the world. This is the Christian parallel, notes Karl-Josef Kuschel, to the kind of laughter we see in Psalm 2, where God laughs at the vain pretensions of humankind in trying to come out from under the sovereign reign of God. Resurrection, he argues, is as an expression of God's laughter at death: 'And only in this way can we understand the cry of jubilation into which Paul breaks out in his First Letter to the Corinthians: "Death is swallowed up in victory. Death, where is your sting? Grave, where is your victory?" (15:54f.) What is that if not Easter jubilation, Easter laughter?"[16]

Whether some of our jokes are up to the task of eliciting this kind of resurrection laughter is a moot point. I have tried a few over the years, and to be honest, whilst they have raised a laugh, to me they fall way short of the divine comedy of that first Easter morning. Nevertheless, I like the idea that the first thing we do on Easter morning, along with the traditional Easter shout of 'Christ is Risen, He is Risen indeed,' is to laugh death in the face. Furthermore, I like the idea that when Jesus said there will be time enough to fast, he was not referring to the rolling centuries of the church, but specifically to that period between Good Friday and Easter Sunday, when the disciples mourned the loss of the bridegroom.[17] And the reason I like this interpretation is not because it lets me off the hook when it comes to fasting, but because I have never been convinced that fasting sits comfortably with the main thrust of Jesus' message: namely, that the Kingdom of God is a party.[18]

Again, this is not an argument for frivolity, nor for the abandonment of spiritual disciplines. On the contrary, such is the licentiousness of our day that we cannot possibly conceive of vital Christianity without disciplines, however awkward we Protestants might feel about that. I would be the first to argue that long-term post-baptismal catechesis is one of the most urgent tasks the church faces in this next generation.[19] But for all our attempts at serious-minded Christianity and radical discipleship, let us never forget that it is all about joy.[20] As a group of New Testament scholars concluded when they came to the end of their deliberations: the hallmark of Christian spirituality is joy – a joy that does not circumvent suffering, but arises precisely from within it.

Indeed, the greatest expressions of joy I have witnessed in my life have often been among those who have nothing, whereas the most miserable people I have met have often been among those who have everything. The Christian community of Nueva Esperanza in Colombia, who sat me down in the sanctuary of their makeshift church so that they could tell me the tragic story of the displacement of their farming community by terrorists (including the assassination of their pastor), was the same community that was able to laugh uproariously, earlier that day, at a little boy who was chasing a pig out of the compound. One seemed to allow for the other. It never occurred to them that joy was forbidden. Joy was present in the midst of suffering. And the reason it was present was because its source came from their hope in Christ and not their fate in society. As the apostle Peter puts it in the first chapter of his first letter to the churches:

> In his great mercy he has given us new birth into a living hope through the resurrection of Jesus Christ from the dead, and into an inheritance that can never perish, spoil or fade, kept in heaven for you who though faith are shielded by God's power until the coming of the salvation that is ready to be revealed in the last time. *In this you greatly rejoice though for a little while you may have had to suffer grief in all kinds of trials. These have come so that your faith – of greater worth than gold, which perishes even though refined by fire – may be proved genuine and may result in praise, glory and honour when Jesus Christ is revealed.*[21]

The ability to hold together joy and suffering is all to do with spiritual humility. Unlike us suburbanites, who seem to think that this world owes us a living, in the poor communities of places like Colombia there exists a greater eschatological realism. Along with David Bentley Hart they admit to a provisional dualism – even if they cannot articulate it as such.[22] In other words, they realise that this world in its present mess is not it; that in so many ways evil is still rampant if not reigning. But strangely enough, this realism about how awful things can get in this world does not stifle laughter, but rather permits it – as a kind of protest, if you will. As Jean-Jacques Suurmond puts it: 'Over against the inescapable fate of tragedy stands the unpredictable surprise of comedy. Humour stakes its money on what is good and is still to come and is thus an act of opposition to the absurdity of evil.'[23]

The one who laughs does not seek to deny the suffering of the world, nor make light of it. Humour must constantly remain open to suffering lest it become superficial and frivolous. We must agree with Rabbi Jonathan Wittenberg when he says, 'No, we cannot entirely fill our mouths with laughter in this world. It's forbidden to seal our conscience.'[24] How can one be at peace and at ease in a world that can produce Auschwitz? How can we fully laugh when children are dying of malnutrition? It is not laughter that we need, worse still entertainment, but action. As we noted earlier, the great injustices of the world should elicit from us anger not levity. However, rather than allowing suffering to completely overwhelm us, laughter somehow subverts its ultimacy, allowing us to see that evil can never have the last word. Yes, there is such a thing as humour around the bedside of a dying person that is wholly inappropriate and hurtful for those present; and oftentimes the humour is due to a deep uneasiness about being in the presence of something tragic. But sometimes in an unexpected humorous comment or action, as I and other pastors have witnessed many times in hospital visiting, quite the opposite is the case. Somehow in a shared laughter, or humorous observation, the suffering can be transcended for a moment in ways that are deeply liberating for all concerned.[25]

It is as if the laughter connects us to 'the deeper magic', to use Lewis's phrase, that all shall be well; that no matter how awful things are, and no matter how powerful evil seems to be, even so, there is a deeper mystery still, that God has triumphed, and therefore our bodies can rest secure, that we can even rejoice. As Paul puts it in that celebrated passage about hope: '*And we rejoice in the hope of the glory of God. Not only so, but we also rejoice in our sufferings, because we know that suffering produces perseverance; perseverance, character; and character, hope. And hope does not disappoint us, because God has poured out his love into our hearts by the Holy Spirit, whom he has given us.*'[26] Suffered things are indeed learned things. The depth of our joy is inextricably related to our ability to embrace it.

Holy Humour

As a preacher I have my fair share of sermon illustrations and not a few of them relate to pious communities. There is something about the incongruity of piety and crudity that makes for good jokes. One of the stories I love most is the one about the Abbot on his sick bed. He was a holy man and venerated as such by the monks of the community who had gathered around the bedside of their leader to hear his last dying words. Surely in his last moments he would impart to them some divine wisdom that would ensure the survival of the community after his departure. He did not disappoint them. Turning to his devoted followers, desperate as they were to hear one final word of wisdom from the great man, he uttered the immortal words: 'I could murder a cold beer.'

I told this story once in a sermon I gave as a visiting preacher in a nearby church. No one laughed! Maybe it was the way I told it. When it comes to jokes, timing is everything. But I suspect the reason they didn't laugh was actually more to do with their own piety: their inability to marry holiness and humanity in the way that I have tried to outline in these last few chapters. In fact, not only did they struggle to appreciate the conjunction of holiness and humour, my guess is that they would have struggled with the whole range of human emotions that I have covered in this section of the book. As with many suburbanites, their Christianity has ended up a decidedly passionless affair. But if our churches are to engage in mission, not to mention reflect the sheer humanity of the incarnate God, then this will have to change. There is nothing virtuous about suburban mediocrity. In fact, there is much wrong with it. It is about as poor an advert for the faith as ever there was. We may cite worse periods in the history of the church, like the Inquisition, but as far as Jesus is concerned lukewarmness is far more sickening.

What I would like to explore in part three is how the church might overcome this cult of the mediocre, both in its understanding of leadership and then in its understanding of community. In order for a more primitive, dare I say more biblical, piety to emerge, not only are there emotional taboos to overcome, but also ecclesiastical norms: ways in which the contemporary church has substituted style for substance; technique for relationships; and worst of all, substituted safety for mission. Indeed, I am reminded of something Morris Berman said in this regard. Speaking of the long-term decline of western civilisation he prophesies that 'Instead of classics we shall have best-sellers; instead of genius, technique. Real thought will be supplanted by information. Security will fade and catastrophe will ensue. Culture will become increasingly debased, emptied of content, until a reaction or catharsis will finally take place.'[27]

Actually, this is not so much prophecy as present-day reality. And what I want to do in the subsequent chapters, ambitious as it may sound, is outline how such a reaction might occur, how such a catharsis might come about in the very heart of the church. And where I want to start is by celebrating the uniqueness of place. For only when we embrace the sheer oddity of the people with whom we have been called to live our lives will we be able to get free of the plasticity of our modern world and enter into the kingdom of God. Only when we climb down from the utopianism of so much of our modern vision and embrace the actual places and people that we have been called to live among will we be able to truly love.

PART THREE

ECCLESIASTICAL PRIMITIVISM

Seven

For the Love of Place

He who loves his dream of a community more than the Christian community itself becomes a destroyer of the latter, even though his personal intentions may be ever so honest and earnest and sacrificial.

Dietrich Bonhoeffer, *Life Together*

Like most pastors I have had the opportunity to travel. It has been my joy and privilege to encounter the church in all kinds of different locations across the globe. I have preached to a tiny congregation on the Hebridean island of Tiree, with the noise of the waves crashing against the rocks outside; enjoyed the hospitality of a Baptist deacon, his wife and seven daughters following an evening service in the small Romanian town of Alesd; visited six churches in one evening with a missionary friend of mine in the displaced community of Monte Libano in northern Colombia; and seen the church in some of the most remote regions of Andhra Pradesh, India. Each place has been utterly fascinating. And as I began to suggest at the end of part two, primitive piety, whatever else it is, represents a delight in the sheer particularity of location. At a time of increasing cultural homogeneity, a more primitive kind of approach draws out for the congregation exactly what it is that makes this setting unique. When the Spirit speaks to the seven churches of Asia Minor, he uses local knowledge of the places in order to make his point. The image of the lukewarm waters of Laodicea is not some hackneyed preacher's illustration but an immersion on the part of the Spirit into the particularity of place. The prophetic message – when it comes – is not an off-the-peg, one-size-fits-all message, but rather a tailor-made utterance that pays attention to all the idiosyncrasies, good and bad, of this actual congregation. In fact, it may well be that the *angel of the church* that is addressed in each of the seven letters is not an actual angel, or even an apostle, but perhaps what we might call the genius or personality of the church: namely, that which makes this church uniquely this church.[1]

The great travesty of 'church growth' books, of course, is that they treat every church the same. Apply these principles, they say, and your church will grow, as if growth could take place outside of the intensely local context that every church finds itself in. What transpires is ecclesiastical pornography on a grand scale. Instead of loving the actual church which is called my congregation, we surf the net for a congregation of my fantasies. In contrast, when Paul begins his letter to the Corinthians, for example, what we discover is not a systematic theology, nor some abstract sermonising, but pastoral theology at its best: the gospel applied to the concrete and unique context of this actual church at this actual time in this actual place. Indeed, the counter-intuitive message of the crucified Messiah, of power made perfect through weakness, which is the message of both of Paul's letters to the Corinthians, can only truly be understood against the backcloth of this context, because of course it is in Corinth of all places that the precise opposite – power and wisdom – was honoured. In the midst of a culture that prizes image and size – which is what makes Corinthians so contemporary, of course – surely one of the things the apostle is urging his congregation to realise is that the gospel plays itself out more often than not in 'the weak things of this world.' Set aside the grandiose visions of the super-apostles with their impressive credentials; true apostolicity works from the back of the queue not the front, in the often inauspicious setting of an actual congregation. Apart from this, we who are called to pastoral ministry have nothing else to recommend us. 'You yourselves are our letter,' says Paul.[2]

A Brand New World

Love of place and context is not easy to do in the suburbs. Such is the ubiquitous nature of corporate branding: Starbucks, McDonalds, Gap, Next, Monsoon, Vodafone, Vision Express,

Waterstones – to name but a few – that suburbia, by definition, is often a flight from the peculiarities and singularities of geography. One High Street looks like another. In fact, in suburbia there is every chance that one residential road looks like another. My grief over seeing a cherry tree opposite our house lopped down a number of years ago was not so much a wistful nostalgia for trees. It had become diseased and was beyond redemption. What grieved me most was that the loss of the tree further increased my sense of the flatness of everything – a flatness that if we are not careful soon begins to infect our churches. In fact, the blandness I talked about earlier in terms of worship, can be attributed to some degree to this rapacious tendency in modern suburbanisation to eradicate the particularity of place, and offer instead, as Bunting puts it in *The Plot*: 'a cultural no man's land homogenized by new technologies of entertainment, mobility and consumerism.'[3]

I am aware, of course, that one's disdain for the blandness of the suburbs can end up as a form of snobbery, even as one's love for the countryside can be nothing more than sheer escapism. The fact of the matter is, I am a beneficiary of the convenience of suburban living. Furthermore, I have never lived on a farm. As Bunting notes of those who, like her father, bought a plot of land in North Yorkshire just after the war as an expression of protest against the monotonous spread of suburbia in the South-East: 'In this panic about the new urbanization, there were strong streaks of misogyny, misanthropy and snobbery.'[4] Yet, for all this, he was definitely on to something. Like the Cistercians, whose Abbeys in North Yorkshire served as the inspiration for his own chapel, Bunting's father understood that there is such a thing as spiritual geography – that place matters.[5] Just as the psalmist describes place by using all the metaphors of God's own armour – 'Ephraim is my helmet, Judah my sceptre, Moab is my washbasin, upon Edom I toss my sandal, over Philistia I shout in triumph'[6] – so we who call ourselves followers of Jesus *of Nazareth* must learn to delineate a faith that is respectful of the divine significance of the place given to us.

This love of place, of particularity, is one of the reasons why I couldn't wait to take my first wedding. One of the things I had always wanted to say was: 'Jesus was himself a guest at a wedding in *Cana of Galilee*, and by his Spirit he is with us now,' because what it does is root the universality of presence with the singularity of place. In a culture which has bowdlerised space, where history has been tarmacked over to make way for the latest multi-story, then primitive piety is about uncovering the peculiarity of the local.[7] At a time when churches are about as indistinct as they can be from each other, programmed to the same 'church growth' strategies, and the same evangelistic initiatives, then primitive piety is about celebrating the genius of this actual church, with all its local particularity. Piety is not about the spiritualising of the gospel; we call that kind of abstracting Gnosticism, and it is rife in our culture. Instead, from the very beginning, the gospel is about immersion into parish, feeling the texture of what goes on, and, above all else, honouring its soul. Not to respect this is the same as a farmer who simply treats the land as a business entrepreneur, or a sculptor who works against the grain of the wood. Sooner or later the land will reject such brutalisation. The art of ministry is to submit to the wood, to allow it to shape our understanding.

In the classic novel *The Diary of a Country Priest*, by Georges Bernanos, such respect for place is critical. How could it be otherwise? What else would draw a young priest fresh out of seminary to a quiet backwater village deep in the heart of the French countryside? Certainly not opportunism; rather, it was his reverence for the field that God assigned him; a respect for the spirituality and sacredness of geography. 'My parish! The words can't be spoken without a kind of soaring love . . . But as yet the idea behind them is so confused. I know that my parish is a reality, that we belong to each other for all eternity; it is not a mere administrative fiction, but a living cell of the everlasting Church.'[8]

Not only does the young cure celebrate the particularity of place but also the specificity of persons – their peculiarity even. In an age when image is everything, when one teenager looks like another, when brand names take precedence over originality, when even our churches homogenise into a colourless mass, then primitive piety is an attempt to retrieve the cult of the individual.

As Morris Berman says: 'In terms of a future renewal much of it will depend on a commitment to individualism, something that has been much maligned in recent years . . . the more individual the activity is and the more out of the public eye, the more effective it is likely to be in the long run.'[9]

He is right. For all our commitment to the body of Christ, to the communitarian nature of our faith, what we must never allow is for this to transmute into bland conformism. Community is not about the suppression of individuality, but rather the expression of it. The church, of all places, is where our originality should be affirmed, not crushed – where we learn to individuate even as we learn to sacrifice. To be sure there is a form of individualism that is nothing more than narcissism: self-expression of the worst kind. But what this must not be confused with is that expression of individualism where we celebrate that with which God has uniquely endowed us. It is one thing to rail against the obsession with personal image. A culture that is constantly obsessing over matters of appearance is a culture that has traded substance for style – and is as guilty as anything for the bland homogeneity we now see in our consumer world. What we must not demolish, however, is the image of God in which each one of us has been made: what the poet Gerard Manley Hopkins calls 'inscape'.

Hopkins developed the idea of inscape from the medieval Franciscan, Duns Scotus – in fact he even wrote a poem in praise of Scotus, for it was Scotus, as we noted earlier, who freed up Hopkins to delight in the wonder of creation without feeling guilty all the time. Indeed, Scotus was a man ahead of his time. Philosophically it is Scotus who began to develop the notion of individuation from which Hopkins develops his concept of inscape: in other words, that each person or thing has a certain thisness; that which makes that person who he or she is. One of the best examples we have of this concept is in a poem called 'Binsey Poplars' (1879), a poem which describes his own devastation over the felling of the trees.

> My aspens dear, whose airy cages quelled,
> Quelled or quenched in leaves the leaping sun,
> All felled, felled, are all felled.[10]

It is a grief that arises from a profound understanding of the way, as human beings, we can either give utterance to the distinctiveness of created things or instead as with the felling of the poplars, by ten or twelve strokes of havoc 'únselve/The sweet especial seen,' because in the end each mortal thing has a precision, a singularity.

Translate this into spiritual formation and we have for ourselves all the encouragement we need to uncover the individuation that we see in scripture itself – the way in which the Spirit both unites us together as the body of Christ but at the same time individuates the parts of the body to do that which it is uniquely gifted to do.[11] I am not talking here about spiritual gift forms. Rather, I am speaking of a community where each person is valued for who they are. To say that we are 'neither Jew nor Greek, slave nor free, male nor female,'[12] is not to obliterate distinctions for the sake of one big amorphous spiritual mass. Quite the opposite. It is, in fact, to say that the ground is level at the foot of the cross, and therefore my membership in the body of Christ is not dependent on conformity to the dominant group, but on faith in a Jesus who seeks the one over the ninety-nine. Here we are in churches obsessing over the ninety-nine, over ways to get more 'bums on seats', on strategies that target specific socio-economic groups, and here is Jesus passing the time of day with a woman at Jacob's Well in Sychar;[13] Philip the evangelist – he with the four unmarried prophetesses – leaving a rally in Samaria to listen to an Ethiopian eunuch, of all people, travelling in a chariot on the desert road to Gaza;[14] Peter praying for little Dorcas, the dressmaker, during his stay at Simon the Tanner's house in Lydda;[15] Paul relinquishing an open-door opportunity in the harbour town of Troas because his friend Titus hasn't shown up.[16]

Everywhere we look in scripture we are confronted with the scandal of particularity – the gospel itself being the greatest example. We live in a culture that teaches us to abstract, depersonalise, idealise, homogenise, but the incarnation insists on the messiness of the whole thing. We think macro, the Bible thinks micro. We prefer global, the Bible prefers local. We love humanity, the Bible loves people: actual people, who live in actual places, with actual names, and actual churches. Anything less is cowardice.

A Vision to be a Church

Let me think of my own congregation for a moment. It is a fairly large church, located in a very pretty part of a very attractive suburban town. And given the history of the church it would be very easy to idealise this new assignment. After all, Millmead has always been something of a flagship church for the denomination: an influential church in an influential town. But this is not its genius. Its genius lies in something altogether more earthy, such as welcome and hospitality. It is known as a preaching centre. What actually makes it tick is the community life that emanates from the preaching.

This came to a head for me right at the beginning of my relationship with the church, on the occasion of the church meeting where the prospective minister is grilled by the congregation. It was an interesting occasion, to say the least. Strangely, no one asked me about my doctrine of the Trinity. For all they knew I could have been a Unitarian. Instead, the interest was on my vision for the church. Standing before about four hundred church members, someone asked me the inevitable question: 'What is your vision for the church?'

I was ready for this question. Having read my quota of 'church growth' books I understand that vision is central to good leadership. But taking a deep breath, and thinking I had nothing to lose, I replied that I had a vision to be a church. The reply is not original to me. I borrowed it from my good friend, Dave Hansen. What lies behind it is a conviction that the best thing we can do for vision is simply do the things that Christians have done for centuries, trusting that through these simple practices, the church will flourish. At the time, I didn't think it satisfied the questioner at all. But it struck me what an odd question it was to pose to a person who wasn't even living in the town yet. How can a person get a vision for a church he doesn't even know? The idea that one can form a vision for a church without immersing oneself first of all in all the oddity that makes up a church, even a large church, is nonsensical. (Actually, I discovered he was delighted with the answer, tired as he was with grand strategies.)

How we go about forming this community is something of a challenge, for what we discover early on is that the people whom

God has placed us with are a motley crew to say the least, and that the easiest thing is simply to revert to type. Hence, young families gravitate towards young families, young people hang out with young people, and all the while real Christian community remains largely unexplored because the vision of the New Testament is not homogeneity but heterogeneity, in which each one is called to live beyond themselves for the sake of the awkward other. In the world of the New Testament, and in the world of most non-western cultures for that matter, family church does not mean a place where there is a good children's programme, but a diverse community in which all the normal ways we demarcate – young, old, married, single, black, white – are relativised for the sake of the first family of the church.[17] In fact, the less programmatic the better. Although structures can be helpful, so often they become barriers to the kind of serendipity that is found in real, authentic communities.

For instance, it is something of a mantra these days that one cannot create Christian community without small groups. Small group programmes are ubiquitous in the modern church. These days one cannot imagine intimate community without them. But as Josh Myers points out in *The Search to Belong*, small groups are only one form of community life.[18] Alongside small groups we must also recognise the validity of larger social space as well as much more personal space, if we are to truly talk about community. Furthermore, far from building up community, small groups can sometimes be a detriment to community. As Myers notes, small groups often fail even before they have begun for they assume an intimacy that is not there. By predicating the existence of small groups in a church on the need for intimacy – which is often how they are promoted – small groups can stifle, paradoxically, the very thing they want to promote. As Bonhoeffer points out, one cannot have direct intimacy: 'Within the spiritual community there is never, nor in any way, any "immediate" relationship of one to another.'[19] All relationships in the Christian community are mediated through the person of Christ. To pursue intimacy, therefore, as a desired goal in itself, actually has the counter-effect of preventing intimacy. 'Because Christ stands between me and others, I dare not desire direct fellowship with them. As only Christ can speak to me in such a way that I may be saved, so others, too, can be saved only by Christ himself.'[20]

Given the trust we place in small group Christianity, I am aware that much of the above sounds very negative. However, my goal is not to dismantle small groups, but simply to insist that we do not place our trust in them. Given how easy it is for us in the suburbs to revert to formulas and strategies, and also how easy it is for us to idealise the church, my point is to suggest that the best examples of Christian togetherness emerge, paradoxically, from those places where people less self-consciously pursue community and instead get on with the simple task of loving God and loving each other. One can monitor the same kind of irony in the way we do worship. The harder we try, it seems to me, the less we worship. For all the benefits of modern worship bands, contemporary musicianship and overhead screens, the overall effect, if we are not careful, is to turn worship into programme, and to rob the grass-roots of real worship. As with ministry in general, worship professionalises and ceases to be the work of the people. Instead of corporate worship coming from the belly of the congregation, it comes from the sound system.

This became most vivid to me on a trip to Pakistan a few years ago. I arrived the day martial law was declared, so there was a palpable tension in the air that first Sunday morning at First Presbyterian Church, Narlaka, situated in the old Imperial part of Lahore. Throughout the service I half expected some kind of incident – a gunman or something like that – to disturb the service. I recall beginning the service with one eye on the backdoor. But whatever nerves I was feeling that morning were more than overcome by something which I had not anticipated: namely the strength of the worship. Accompanied by simply a sitar and tabla, how the worship worked was that someone would strike up a song, and suddenly, like a great whoosh of energy and feeling, the whole congregation would join in: no overheads, no complicated musical arrangements, no spectators, just raw, heart-felt, passionate, congregational singing, of a kind that I had not heard in a long time. It was so intoxicating, so fresh, so gloriously primal, that at one point I think I was laughing. What was so wonderful about it was not just its indigenous rhythm and language, which in itself was so compelling, but its sheer naivety.

I have been around long enough, and travelled often enough, to know that no church is without problems. And with multiple stories of falls from grace, financial corruption, and even nepotism, the church in Pakistan is no exception. But even so, the worship I experienced was striking and challenging. What the church gave expression to was a kind of worship that we have long since abandoned: worship that is genuinely congregational, rooted in the language of the Bible's own hymnody. Perhaps above all else, it was worship that relies not on modern technology, with its PA and its screens, but on the collective memory of the people: a kind of second orality, to put it technically, that made our own worship seem tame by comparison. Here were people who were not looking to the worship leader to whip up the crowd, nor relying on the mood of the song to stir the emotions. Instead, we had something that arose from the heart of the congregation itself.

Whether we will be able to get back to such simplicity of worship is doubtful. Contemporary worship, as Pete Ward points out, has become something of an industry, and is showing no signs of abating.[21] Without sounding overly critical there are very few songs that have slipped into the corporate memory of the church such that, should the PA break down, or the overhead screen cease to work, we would still be able to worship. And the fact that this is the case ought to be of serious concern, for if it is the case that we are wholly reliant on technology to pull our worship events off, it is likely that we are no longer talking about worship, but about something else.

Again, it is only by travelling, seeing the church in other parts of the world where there are fewer resources, that one becomes aware of the problem – at least that is how it works for me. Instead of coming back from these trips abroad with a sense of superiority at the state of our churches, my usual feeling is that we are decidedly inferior: that somewhere along the line we have substituted performance for passion and, perhaps most pernicious of all, technology for prayer.

I became acutely aware of this disjuncture whilst visiting a small church in rural Romania. We arrived about six o'clock, just as dusk was settling in. There were cows walking down the dirt track towards the centre of the village, geese milling around at the sides of the houses, the smell of the farm everywhere. Right in the middle of the village, as is the case all across Romania, was a large-scale Orthodox church – way out of proportion to the size of the village, with its onion dome and silver cross shimmering in the evening light. It felt like something out of a Tolstoy novel. The Baptist chapel, where I was due to be, was about the only thing incongruous to the Tolstoyan vision: it was built much later than the other buildings in the village, and was not particularly attractive.

The Baptists in Romania are very different, of course, to the Orthodox, as well as to the Catholics. In Herta Müller's bleak – almost Kafkaesque – novel, *Passport*, set in the German Romanian community of the Banat, the night watchman speaks disparagingly of them: 'The ones with the small hats are Baptists. They howl when they pray and their women groan when they sing hymns, as if they were in bed.'[22] Actually, this is a pretty good description. The men really do howl when they pray and the woman really do groan when they sing. But it is not groaning 'as if they were in bed,' as the night watchman mocks, but the groaning of women who have sought God all their lives: lamented during the time of Romania's communist history when faith hung by a thread; prayed through the dramatic events of 1989 when Ceausescu's regime fell; and now interceding as western consumerism begins to encroach upon the piety of the younger generation.

In fact, it is generally agreed that western consumerism has been a far greater threat to the church in Eastern Europe than communism ever was. If the presence of the Secret Police acted as a boon to faith, the effect of the shopping mall has been its erosion. But whereas the church in the west tends to think that some latest strategy or technique will get the job done (because that is how we think in consumer societies) the Christians here know, at the most basic level, that in the end it is prayer that will make the difference. And so they groan. In fact, in many Baptist churches across Romania, the first hour of church on a Sunday is still devoted to prayer; and among the young seminarians there is a very real agreement that what the church in Romania needs at this present time is not some latest fad from North America, but more of the same: urgent, persistent, and heart-felt prayer.

If ever we are to return to this kind of simplicity, perhaps the most important thing of all that needs to happen is for us to relinquish any residual idealism concerning the church. In other words, if we are to have real community then we must accept that a large part of our experience will be living with imperfection. Again, this will not be easy for us suburbanites to do. We live with a sense of ultimacy. Theologically and culturally, we are striving for perfection. What is prosperity all about but that striving for the ultimate experience or that ultimate look? And translated into contemporary faith, so often what we look for in churches is that ultimate worship, or that ultimate experience. But as Bonhoeffer reminds us, in order for us to truly realise community we must die to the dream of it.[23] What we need are not pristine churches, but actual churches; and alongside that we need not so much professional management but impassioned ministry. It is to this that we now turn, before exploring the kind of mission in which such churches might be engaged.

Eight

Passionate Leadership

> It is important for seminaries to impart skills and competencies; it is more important to ignite conviction and courage to lead. The language of facilitation is cool and low risk. The language of priesthood and prophecy and the pursuit of holiness is impassioned and perilous.
>
> Richard Neuhaus, *Freedom for Ministry*

Pastors are a strange breed. Of all the professions, so called, pastors are perhaps the most ill-disciplined. Many are recovering workaholics. Not a few that I know think nothing of working seventy or eighty hours a week. They think nothing of going from one event, such as a funeral, and then to a counselling session, to a leaders' meeting, all in one afternoon and evening. Many of the pastors I know – and I dare say others will say the same about me – so live and breathe the church that it soon becomes difficult for them to know where the church stops and their own life begins. Just about all of the men and women with whom I have worked closely over the years have so felt the mood of the church that their own emotional life can be gauged, pretty much, by whether the church is up or down.

Of course, any professional will tell you – whether they are a nurse, a doctor, a lawyer, or even a footballer (for whom 'being professional' is now something of a mantra) – that this kind of emotional dependency is not good. The golden rule of professionalism, almost by definition, is a certain measure of emotional detachment. Emotion must always be the servant of reason. 'Whether it's the way you conduct yourself in meetings, on the phone, or over email,' notes the 99% tip, 'a well-composed tone is a key component in the way others will perceive you. This is critical in situations involving potential and existing clients, collaborators, partners and financiers; your livelihood and business depend on it.' 'Professionalism,' it goes on to say, 'becomes difficult in work fueled by passion because passion is an emotion. Emotion generates energy, but it also impairs judgement.'[1] According to this criterion most pastors are decidedly unprofessional. Our passionate approach to ministry makes us look very odd indeed alongside the cool, professional approach of the manager. But the more I have reflected on my experience of working with those who tie their emotions so closely to the church, the more I have come to see that although it may not be a very professional way of carrying on, it is a least biblical – apostolic even. Hence, having argued in previous chapters for a greater emotional range in worship as well as everyday life, and having argued for a greater love for the particularity of the place in which we are called to live, I want to argue here for a greater emotional intensity in leadership, both inside and outside the church. I want to argue for it, for it seems to me to be a style of leadership that is commensurate with the very nature of the God who has called us to serve his people. In short, since God is passionate about his people, so those who minister in his name must be.

In stating things thus, I imagine I have already lost some readers. After all, if Christian ministry is to have any credibility in a culture which, frankly, tolerates our existence (or conveniently makes use of us on special occasions when a chaplain is needed), then competency and professionalism will need to subsume any latent passion on our part, lest we be deemed amateurish – or so the argument runs. Indeed, we have witnessed in the last few decades a huge shift of emphasis towards more managerial models of ministry precisely for this reason. Even the therapeutic models of ministry, which have become so much a part of pastoral care in recent decades, evince a similar kind of clinical detachment.[2] The emphasis is less on the adventure of life in the Spirit than it is on the competency of the counsel.

But whilst one can understand this approach, and even admire the way in which the mainstream denominations have set their stall out and sought proper accreditation, the point is that such managerial and therapeutic models of leadership are alien to the world of the Bible. When Paul, for instance, describes his sadness about having to leave the church at Thessalonica, and his subsequent desire to see them again, his is not the cool composed language of the professional minister, but the raw passion of a lover, desperate to see his beloved. It is not enough for him to say that he longs to see them. It is more like a raw primal craving. First he was a gentle mother and an encouraging father to these raw fledgling converts; now he sees himself as an orphan, cut off from his parents, and trying, again and again, to get back to them. This is how Eugene Peterson translates 1 Thessalonians 2:17–20 in *The Message*:

> Do you have any idea how very homesick we became for you, dear friends? Even though it hadn't been that long and it was only our bodies that were separated from you, not our hearts, we tried our very best to get back to see you. You can't imagine how much we missed you! I, Paul, tried over and over to get back, but Satan stymied us each time.[3]

Hardly balanced! In fact, for all the vividness of Peterson's translation, the literal sense is not homesickness, which is visceral enough, but of physical longing – the longing of the lover for the beloved. In other words, what we have here is instinctive love as opposed to institutional duty. Furthermore, if this love for the Christian community at Thessalonica seems to be at the expense of his compatriots in the synagogue, of whom he speaks of in less than loving tones a few verses earlier ('The wrath of God has come upon them at last' – verse 16b), even this is really only the flip side of the same coin; in Romans 9:2, he expresses a wish that he was accursed, cut off, for the sake of his own countrymen. Paul was entirely caught up with the people whom he served. Here there is no half-measure, or emotional holding back, but rather an impassioned dependency.

Interestingly, it was precisely this language of *accursedness* in Romans that provoked one of Fred Craddock's homiletics students to comment: 'How unprofessional!' And I remember noting at the time, listening on cassette to Fred's humorous rendition of the nonchalant young man turning up to his preaching class in his tennis whites, the particular word he used to defame Paul, because it occurred to me even then that this was the heart of the issue. Of course, Paul is unprofessional, because there is something about following Jesus that is, in and of itself, profoundly unprofessional. For all the attempts of Christian leaders to mimic the management skills of the corporate world, the heart of Christian leadership, it must be understood, is not composed rationality, balanced arguments or clever oratory, but, like the gospel we proclaim, raw, womb-like love.[4] The images Paul uses for ministry rise above the dead metaphors of middle-management, with all their guarantees of control, and promote instead the shockingly visceral images of a woman in labour, with all the implications of vulnerability.[5] Contrary to so many popular perceptions of Paul the misogynist, the bigot, the perverter of the simple gospel, we see Paul, like Jesus, plundering these feminine images time and again, and by so doing leaving us with the overwhelming conclusion that leadership has little to do with professional clarity, and everything to do with passion – both for God and for his people.[6] A doctor may be able to do his work dispassionately, but for a minister of Christ it is a sackable offence. When it comes to ministerial credentials, the thing that matters for Paul is not the all-important letter of recommendation, so prized by the super-apostles of his day, with its attestation of rhetorical skill and strategic acumen. As far as Paul is concerned those things are boastful, not to mention worthless. Rather, the thing that matters for Paul – in fact the only thing that validates what he is doing – is the existence and sustenance of an actual letter, namely the church, containing the names and faces of all those who have been made alive in Christ.[7] This is not exactly sensational, for sure, but nonetheless it is the only thing that bears witness to the power of the gospel. As Richard Neuhaus puts it, 'if we have anything to hang on our walls it is not our diplomas but a simple crucifix. Because this is all we have to say for ourselves.'[8]

Conference Christianity

That we don't go this way, and plump instead for the bright lights of celebrity Christianity and big-name conferences is because this is so much the air that we breathe. And that so many

Christian leaders opt for 'church growth' strategies and managerial models of leadership instead of immersing themselves in the life of their congregation is because, frankly, it is far easier to love a programme than it is to love people. At least programmes can't hurt you. But however much we might sympathize with this – and I am utterly convinced this is why pastors adopt programmes – it is vanity all the same. It is a theology of glory, to use Luther's phrase, and not the theology of the cross, because it seeks to root our identity in criteria that we can measure, in models of success, rather than the passion that must always accompany pastoral leadership of a community.[9]

By no means does a commitment to this way of passion excuse unprofessional conduct, any more than it excuses pastoral inefficiency. We ought to expect high standards among those who are called to minister in Christ's name, and leaders at the very least ought to be professionally competent. There is no virtue in professional sloppiness. But if we make professionalism the heart of what we do, and the source of what we pride ourselves on, it is likely we will miss a great deal of what God intended for us when we committed to follow Christ in the church and in the world. After all, Jesus crossed boundaries all the time. The incident with the woman at the well in the fourth chapter of John breaks all the rules of professional conduct. As Herrick and Mann point out, the miracle of resurrection in chapter eleven is driven not by abstract notions of power and authority, but by friendship. Why Jesus wept is simply because that is what we do when we love. Hence, when we also love: when we sit down at a well to listen to a woman's story, or when we weep with the mourners at the graveside of an old man whom we have just buried, we are not violating the norms of professional conduct, nor are we an embarrassment to the denomination that ordained us; instead we are subverting those norms, fulfilling what lies at the very heart of ordination, which is the willingness to risk all on the mercies of God.

At a time when ministerial formation in our seminaries and in our denominations is increasingly driven by the dictates of academic, managerial and professional conduct, my own conviction is that great courage as well as a sense of urgency is now needed in order to recover a more visceral kind of ministry for the church.

The church requires leaders who spurn the latest technique for growth in preference for a fascination with people; leaders who know about issues of health and safety, for sure, but are more interested in the actual communities for whom those policies were intended; and above all, leaders who are less bothered about vision statements and more taken up with ministry. After all, as Viv Thomas reminds us, 'vision from God does not come in neat packages. Confusion and emotion are acceptable parts of the human condition.'[10] When Nehemiah came to Jerusalem, contrary to what our vision gurus might suppose, he did not know immediately what to do. Clarity was not second nature to him. Instead, he wandered among the ruins; he felt the sadness of the people; he sought God as to what to do. But it is precisely in this wandering and praying, weeping and wresting, that real vision forms.

In this sense, we must insist that a large part of leadership formation – whether lay or ordained – is thrashed out in the exigencies of the church rather than the simulated world of conferences. As Eugene Peterson describes them to his fictitious friend Gunner, a new Christian, conferences are 'high in fat, low in protein.'[11] Though there are a few exceptions, where serious reflection takes place on the practice of ministry and the mission of the church, most conferences perpetuate the lie that there is some key out there which will substitute for long-term faithfulness. In fact, I increasingly see the world of conferencing like a simulated world, which in the end does more harm than good. While we are being thrown about, like those simulated airplanes, in the comfy chair of our conference seat, our parishes are crashing. Essential pastoral work gets neglected for what is called leadership development, when actually the best leadership development, as any other century apart from ours will testify, is done in the backyard of one's own parish.

My own conviction is that we ought to call a moratorium on conferences, or at least be more circumspect in our selection of them. Instead, we should learn the lessons that can only be learnt from working at the coal face. Otherwise, a bit like the way the nursing profession has developed its training in the last couple of decades, there is every danger that our pastors emerge from the world of Project Christianity knowing everything about management, but unable to give even a basic pastoral injection. We must insist that those who are called to shepherd the flock actually make those calls to the hospital; turn up at the nursing home; seek out those who have been away from the church for months. For it is there, among our parishioners, that our sermons recover their immediacy. Too many sermons, in my view, are derived from a combination of internet searches and preacher illustration books. For a sermon to really live, and for it to have legitimacy among the congregation, it must eschew these cheap means of grace, and emerge instead from the grittiness of text, Spirit and pastoral realities. At least then it will be honest. By virtue of the sheer earthiness of the language of scripture, and the sheer messiness of lives, the language we then employ will at least be stripped clean of the platitudes that so often attach to conference-style Christianity, and come forth as raw, gutsy and gospel.

Conference Christianity trades in ultimacy. Like some versions of Christian counselling, it propagates the myth of the land of 'perpetual holiday'. Given the right techniques and dynamic leadership this world – which is, oddly, always just over the horizon – is promised to us as a reality. Primitive leadership, on the other hand, rejects this bland optimism, preferring to do its work between the intersection of the old world and the new, which is actually where our congregations live. Call these leaders pessimists if you like, unambitious and lacking in ideals. On more than one occasion I have been accused of this myself. But as Roger Scruton notes: 'Paradoxical though this may seem, [. . .] such people are more likely to exhibit public spirit, local patriotism and the core impulses of *agape* or neighbour-love than those who entertain themselves with exultant hopes for a human future.'[12] The reason they are more likely to do so is because they have reconciled themselves to the realities of the people and the place they have been called to serve. Conference Christianity, as I call it, requires no commitment on our part, whereas primitive leadership, like all primitive religion, roots us in incarnational realities, in those 'little obediences' that go into making up the kingdom of God.

Future Leader

That such a form of leadership might emerge in our churches is largely dependent on the kind of theology they inhabit. Churches get the leaders they deserve. A church that seeks to be on the success curve, disdainful of the tension that is found in Paul's theology for instance, will inevitably root around for a leader that is likewise uncomplicated: a rancher rather than a pastor, to use the current terminology. A church that wants to engage in gospel ministry, on the other hand, will wait for a leader who is suspicious of these grandiose plans, preferring instead to follow the often unpredictable and unscheduled ways of the Spirit.

The contrast is not either/or, of course. The pastoral instinct to shepherd a flock and the evangelistic impulse to gather a harvest of souls ought not to be mutually exclusive. Jesus was able to allow both metaphors of ministry to sit alongside each other. Looking out on the crowds as 'sheep without a shepherd,' he then begins to talk about the fact that 'the harvest is plentiful, but the workers are few.'[13] At the same time as Paul expressed a love for all the churches, he was actively engaged in proclaiming the gospel all the way from Jerusalem to Illyricum.[14] In other words, just because we want to see the gospel grow numerically does not mean we have sold out to Madison Avenue. Churches should release their pastors to do some of this work, or at least to have time to hang out on the margins. It strikes me as a very Jesus-centered thing to do. But neither must we disdain, as so often happens when the church thrusts out evangelistically, or prophetically, the routine pastoral life of the church as somehow second best, less than radical. Once we strip away the effete, somewhat dainty images of the pastoral setting, defamiliarising ourselves with the lambs gamboling over the lush green hills, we discover that pastoral ministry is about as prophetic as it gets. The various decisions that pastors make on a daily basis amidst the mess of the sheep pen are precisely the kind of judgements that revolutionise the world.

Again, in comparison to the bright lights of the conference platform, the primitive and intensely personal world of the shepherd seems obsolete. Alongside the new apostolic leaders with their hectic schedules, the institutional life of the pastor cuts a very sorry figure indeed. But actually it is just here, in the routine maintenance of life, that the mission of God often finds its greatest growth. Counselling a woman through the issues of an abortion may not sound very dynamic, anymore than listening to someone come out about their sexual orientation. Often these conversations take place one to one, can be very exhausting, and rarely yield easy answers. But we do them nonetheless because, as Stanley Hauerwas points out, these pastoral conversations, which pastors engage in on a routine basis, are nothing less than the building blocks of a new kingdom.[15] Drawing alongside a young adolescent and listening to the particulars of their broken life may not be very time-effective, nor contribute to a numerically successful youth work. But as Andrew Root points out, it is congruent with the incarnate Christ and with hope for the future. Youth work, he goes on to say (by which we mean this relatively recent way of demarcating teenagers from the rest of the church), is not about influencing young people for Jesus. That way lies manipulation, because more often than not it is predicated on the need of the church to have a thriving youth department. Rather, the heart of youth work is found precisely in the midst of those long-term pastoral relationships, where even if it becomes clear that there is no obvious or immediate solution to whatever problem there is, it matters not, since there is something about the person themselves, the uniqueness of their life, that merits our time and attentiveness. Ministry is not so much about the 'how', but about the 'who': 'about the person of Christ who meets the persons of the world as the incarnate, crucified and resurrected One.'[16] Short of this, ministry ends up as an exercise in evangelical conformity, wrapped up as programme participation or camp registration. And when young people fail to respond to that, as so often they do, what happens, argues Root, is that the church feels justified in its neglect of a great many adolescents. In actual fact, he continues, 'it may well be that the reason they don't trust our offer of friendship is that they intuitively know that we are not willing to see, hear and accompany them in their deepest suffering. We have offered them trips to Disneyland, silly games and "cool" youth rooms, not companionship in their darkest nights, their scariest of hells.'[17]

To use a phrase coined by James Olthuis, I would like to describe this kind of ministry as 'withing'.[18] In contrast to the somewhat clinical, often impersonal, designations of counselor/counselee, with all the attendant pressures of fixing lives, or in contrast to the somewhat managerial models of ministry, where people exist for the sake of the vision, Christian ministry is the simple thing of 'withing': an immersion into the messiness of life. To minister in Christ's name is to abandon the pristine world of success-driven suburbia, and instead to discern the contours of grace in the most unlikely people. It is to jettison the controlled, and often cliché-ridden world of performance-related work, and instead to take risks. And finally, lest ministry is reduced to nothing more than a series of truisms, ministering in Christ's name is to relinquish the need for recognition, and embrace instead the obscurity of the cross. For even Christ, as Paul says, did not consider his equality with God something to be exploited, but made himself nothing.[19] Rejecting the lure of relevance, power and sensationalism, he chartered the way of prayer, trust and obedience.[20] Such a way is counter-intuitive, to be sure. It sounds like resignation. But what Easter Sunday confirms, in surprising and unexpected ways, is that this is the way of God. Furthermore, it lies at the heart of mission, because once we reject the way of success, of numerical growth, then we become vulnerable at last to the very people Jesus is reaching on the margins of our communities. In such a scenario, evangelism ceases to be a competition with other churches over the same shrinking pool of believers, which is too often the case, and becomes a genuine engagement in mission to those who otherwise would not enter our lives. It is to this mission that we now turn as the logical end point of primitive faith: not mission under the rubric of recruitment but via the image of hospitality.

Nine

Untamed Hospitality

I remember a house where all were good to me
God knows, deserving no such thing:
Comforting smell breathed at very entering,
Fetched fresh, as I suppose, off some sweet wood.

Gerard Manley Hopkins, *In the Valley of the Elwy*

The Guildford Magazine is not one I subscribe to. Apart from anything else it is full of adverts. But since I was waiting to have my hair cut, and since it seemed to be the only magazine on the table that was seemly for a Baptist minister to read, I started to browse through. Somewhere in the middle was an interview with French chef, Raymond Blanc, whose chain patisserie, Maison Blanc, was just a stone's throw from where I was sitting. For a while it was my wife's favourite place for coffee. With all the barbers still preoccupied, I began to read.

It was an interesting article, covering – among other things – his early experiences of working in England, the importance of eating together, and also a tip on how to make good Welsh cakes. (Having been weaned on Welsh cakes as a young boy, with vivid memories of Mrs Jenkins' pantry always being stocked full of the heavenly manna, I was particularly keen to see what he had to say on the matter.) But having digested that, it was more his clinical views on how businesses survive recession that proved the most compelling as well as disturbing part of the article. There in bold font, lifted out of the main body of the text, was the chilling sentence: 'A recession can be a huge cleansing process. If you are not good enough the market will tell you.'[1]

Now, anyone with any business acumen will say that this is exactly right. This is precisely what happens in recession. Good businesses survive. Those that are built on the sand are washed away in the storm of the economic cycle. And having seen my father's steel business weather the recession of the eighties, at a time when many manufacturing industries simply disappeared, I know that this is no mean feat. But why I found the quote chilling, and why I still ponder its implications, is because (quite apart from the quasi-divine status accorded to the market) the kind of social Darwinism that this 'survival of the fittest' represents is the exact opposite of what Jesus was about, namely God's hospitality to the stranger. If suburban piety is an exercise in keeping the stranger out, demarcating the successful over and against the failures of the capitalist enterprise, then primitive piety is about suspending these categories and recognising instead the shocking earthiness of the body of Christ.

Eating with Sinners and Tax Collectors

Scholars are divided in their opinion on many aspects of Jesus' ministry. Why else would they be scholars? But one thing they are all agreed upon is that Jesus 'ate with sinners and tax collectors': in other words, the very people who had been flushed out by the system – the religious system that is. At a time when Israel was increasingly defining itself by 'the politics of holiness',[2] protecting the faith against paganism by intensifying the requirements of the law, Jesus comes along and in a somewhat avant-garde manner[3] (and fully aware of the old adage that 'you are who you eat with'), starts defining Israel by a very different kind of politics by offering hospitality to all the wrong kinds of people. Jesus challenged his disciples to resist the temptation to invite to our meals only those who can return in kind – that is easy – but rather to invite those who, by the very nature of things, would never get a look in: namely, the poor, the crippled, the lame and the blind.[4] For Jesus is working out a very different politics to that of the Pharisees: what we might call a 'politics of compassion', at the centre of which is not your typical reciprocity – you invite me and I will invite you – but what some have referred to as *untamed* hospitality. In other words, Jesus models a gift of hospitality that goes beyond the bounds of social convention and middle-class idealism, and embraces an altogether more messy social arrangement.

How subversive this might be can be deduced by the dominant images of hospitality that prevail in our culture at the moment, such as 'corporate hospitality'. Whilst there are, undoubtedly, some good things that take place under the canopy of corporate hospitality, and whilst I admit that I too have been the beneficiary of it over the years, it is undoubtedly true that corporate hospitality is to a large extent driven by the market, and for the most part ends up excluding rather than embracing. In fact, just the other day I received an email in my junk box entitled 'the definitive hospitality experience', inviting me to MINT polo in the park: a fast moving, high octane version of polo – the polo equivalent to 20/20 cricket. That it was labelled hospitality suggested to me that I might be welcome, but when I scrolled down it was quite clear that the hosts, the Hurlingham Club, saw the event as anything but inclusive of people like me. 'Set in 42 acres of beautiful gardens,' it posted, 'overlooking the river Thames in Fulham, this exclusive, members only club, will host hospitality guests on all 3 days.' Needless to say, it was for sums of money that only the exclusive set can afford. In others words, it was not hospitality at all, but corporate entertaining. Elizabeth Newman notes various other distortions of hospitality in our culture: sentimental hospitality, privatized hospitality, homeless hospitality as well as hospitality as a mode of marketing.[5]

We come to the church and hope for something beyond this, but sadly things are not always much better. Here the problem is not so much corporate hospitality – even if, at times, the church is guilty of simply providing entertainment – but 'tamed hospitality': a kind of hospitality that retreats to the safe world of loving those who have the ability and the means to love us back. This is alright as far as it goes, for it is important that we have a circle of friends (I write this just after a most enjoyable evening with some close friends at *Jamie's Italian* in Guildford). But to be a disciple of Jesus requires us to go one step further: a kind of *untamed* hospitality that embraces the mess as well as the pristine; that dignifies the poor as well as the rich; and above all, lets Jesus decide who it is that forms our community. After all, the judgement will be determined, according to that stunning passage at the end of Matthew's gospel, by what we have done with 'the least of these brothers and sisters of mine'.[6] And although this phrase probably refers in the first instance to the disciples of Jesus – 'these brothers and sisters *of mine*' – it has a wider frame of reference than that, and underlines the very same thing that we are on about here: that at the heart of authentic faith is a willingness to work on the margins. For Jesus, holiness is nothing other than this. What I mean is: holiness and showing hospitality to strangers are not two mutually exclusive categories. As Luke Bretherton points out, hospitality *is* holiness. How we receive the poor and the downtrodden is the measure, according to Jesus, and according to the prophets, of how holy we really are.[7]

The danger in pursuing this kind of hospitality is that it can come across as ever so patronising: like we are doing the poor a favour. 'Does he take sugar?' is a phrase that comes to mind at this point, as the epitome of middle-class condescension, and the very worst of what it means to be charitable. For it to be truly untamed hospitality there has to be a recognition that we come to the table as equals. As Bretherton points out, with reference to the ethics of the kingdom in the banquet parables, the giving of Aristotle's magnanimous man serves 'to reinforce the superior status of the giver and his self-sufficiency and autonomy. By contrast, the host of the parable does not remain self-sufficient. He actively pursues relationships with others, and it is pursued in such a way that he is rendered vulnerable to rejection, while the recipients are blessed by participation in the feast.'[8] In short, he needs them, even as he identifies with them. Not only does he give to the poor, but he receives from them. His offer of solidarity with the poor finds its source in his own need for a party. Hence, in the kingdom of God, it becomes impossible to discern who is the host and who are the guests. As Luther said in his dying words: 'We are all beggars, it is true.'

The L'Arche communities, founded by Jean Vanier, are perhaps the best testimony we have of this kind of thing. Formed at a time when there was still a lot of stigma attached to disability, Vanier and others (the Catholic priest, Henri Nouwen, being the most famous), began to explore a different way of approaching such people. Tempting as it is to look down on the disabled as inferior, and worthy of our charity, the experience of living together, says Vanier, is that we discover the brokenness within each one of us. 'People come to our communities because they want to serve the poor,' he notes. 'They will only stay once they have discovered that they themselves are the poor.'[9]

We can deny this of course. Vanier observes his own compulsive drive to achieve, to be busy and to be on top. 'Elitism is the sickness of us all. We all want to be on the winning team.'[10] But if we allow it to, living and working with those who are disabled, as I did for a number of years when I was a student, can erode our sense of competency and teach us to walk a different way. The disabled become our tutors. Once someone asked Nouwen why it was he spent so much time with Adam, a severely disabled young man whom Nouwen was assigned to early on in his life at the Daybreak community. He could be getting on with so many other important things, the questioner implied. Nouwen was shocked: 'Don't you see that Adam is my friend, my teacher, my spiritual director, my counselor, my minister?'[11] Beginning each day with Adam was a reminder of his own disability,[12] and the need to conceive the day not around what he could achieve but what he could gratefully receive. Adam was a prophetic sign of a different kingdom, in which we are accepted not for what useful purpose we can serve, but accepted for who we are. Nouwen writes,

> Living close to Adam and the others brought me closer to my own vulnerabilities. While at first it seemed quite obvious who was handicapped and who was not, living together day in and day out made the boundaries less clear. Yes, Adam, Rose, and Michael couldn't speak, but I spoke too much. Yes, Adam and Michael couldn't walk, but I was running around as if life was one emergency after another. Yes, John and Roy needed help in their daily tasks, but I, too, was constantly saying, 'Help me, help me.' And when I had the courage to look deeper, to face my emotional neediness, my inability to pray, my impatience and restlessness, my many anxieties and fears, the word 'handicap' started to have a whole new meaning.[13]

Christmas at Mildmay

I experienced this very same thing one Christmas, when a number of us from the church participated in a carol service at the Mildmay hospice for AIDS patients, where Bekah, one of our church members, worked as a music therapist. Mildmay has a history of Christian mission going all the way back to the mid-Victorian era when it opened to treat cholera victims in the East End of London. So when it was reconceived in the eighties as a hospice for AIDS patients, it was drawing on a long tradition of compassion to the poor. That celebrated moment in 1989 when Princess Diana visited the hospice – reached out, in front of the world's media, and shook the hand of one of the patients – still remains one of the pivotal episodes in our understanding of social justice. Like Jesus, she demonstrated that in the politics of compassion holiness is not contaminated by contact with the shame of sickness – therein lies hypocrisy. Rather, shame is healed by contact with holiness.

At the carol service that day there was a whole range of day care patients who, like the eight of us from the church, had trudged through the snow to make it to the event. For one young woman, from Ghana, it was her last day at the hospital. Her treatment had come to a successful end and she was being discharged. For another older lady, originally from Liberia I recall, this would be her only Christmas celebration as she had no other community with whom to celebrate. Still another, an older man from Chad, said he didn't believe in Christmas at all. But since it was the only thing on offer that morning he was still happy to sing along to the carols we were about to lead.

As we went round the room, gently enquiring as to where people were from, and genuinely keen to understand what kind of people had gathered that cold December morning in a day care room in Shoreditch, it was clear that here was a most unusual and unlikely kind of congregation. But instead of feeling above this, it occurred to a number of us that morning that we were not so different ourselves. For sure, we had acquired some badges of achievement, and no doubt had a good deal more support systems in place, by way of family and friends. Furthermore, we were most definitely from the dominant social and ethnic group in our country. But despite that we were the same. Whether it was sharing music together, the increasing intermingling as the service went on, the mince pies and coffee together afterwards, or whether it was just our own sense of frailty, our shared humanity was more apparent than our differences. Like Query in Graham Greene's *A Burnt-Out Case*, who finds himself helping in a leper colony in Africa after running away from his life as a successful architect, what was more apparent to us that morning was not our superiority to those who were in hospital but our affinity.[14]

The only disappointment for me about that morning at the Mildmay was that at the end of the carol service we were invited into an adjoining room to partake in a wonderful Christmas lunch – separate from the patients. I imagine the reason for this was partly lack of space and also an awareness on the part of the staff that we needed a break. It was a kindly gesture, but disappointing all the same because as Brendan Bryne puts it, 'The banquet image accurately conveys what the kingdom of God is all about – not power and dominion, like the kingdoms of this world – but gifting and honoring human beings with the superabundant hospitality of God.'[15] Eating together that day would have been a fitting end to a service that was in its own small way a window onto that kind of world.

Welcoming the Stranger

As I write this, some people in our church are exploring precisely this vision: offering to the homeless people of Guildford, of which there are surprisingly many, a table where they can eat together. Still others run a programme whereby teams of young people go into some of the rougher parts of town to do garden and home make-overs. But it is not that we need a programme to do this; simply that we need to be open and available to people. For sure, Jesus had an agenda. In his very first sermon at Nazareth he announced a manifesto that might best be described as a kind of Jubilee.[16] But what we then witness in the rest of the gospel is a delightful casualness in Jesus' ministry, an almost *ad hoc* approach to the needs of the world. The systematic fulfilling of an agenda is not as important to Jesus as particular attentiveness to the personal: whether it is Peter's mother-in-law who has a fever; a woman who has been haemorrhaging for the past twelve years; a young boy who is fitting.[17] In the gospels, these are all uniquely presented. Not one of them is a statistic. In what must surely be the epitome of any theology of hospitality, Jesus has that incredible ability to stop whatever he is doing for the sake of this one person in front of him, as if no one else mattered.

To be on the receiving end of such hospitality is dazzling. Who has not felt ennobled when someone gives you their full attention? For all the books on child-rearing, all the formulas for growing kids God's way, maybe Ross Campbell is right: all a child wants in the end is that we look them in the eye when they speak to us, and give them our time. For it is then that we really know that we are loved.[18] But in order for this to happen we will need to receive the world on its own terms, and not on the basis of how we would like it to be. If we have an aversion to the ambiguities of life, even the ambiguities of our own soul, we will find this kind of hospitality difficult. As Christine Pohl puts it, 'Offering hospitality requires that we allow a place for uncertainty, contingency and human tragedy.'[19]

And thus it is that real hospitality will not be possible in the suburbs until we strike at the heart of suburbia's avoidance of such things – the various ways in which we cocoon ourselves from the suffering of the world – and find courage instead to expose ourselves to the vagaries of human existence, wherever we might find it.[20] And it's not as if we have to flee the suburbs to do this. There is enough suffering right under our noses, if we care to look. But as long as success stories feature as the staple diet of our church testimonies, and as long as churches conceive their mission on the basis of impacting influential people, or worse still celebrities, then my guess is that our communities will be nothing more than the fellowship of the winners, rather than the fellowship of the broken, which is what they were called to be. We will be welcoming alright; many churches I know have a good reputation for being welcoming; it is one of the hallmarks of growing churches, so we are told, and therefore something we are alert to. But to be welcoming is not necessarily the same as hospitality. Indeed, it could well act as a smokescreen because while we are congratulating ourselves on our friendliness, the gospel summons to open our homes to the stranger in our midst goes unheeded. Christianity is not reciprocal love: nice people inviting over other nice people. Any rank pagan can do that. Christian faith goes beyond that, offers something 'more than', to use the words of Jesus.[21] And what we see in the love of the awkward other, the stranger, and even our enemies, is a sign of the gratuitous love that God has for us.

Uncomfortable Friends

It is Phyllis McGinley who ought to have the last word here. As we noted in the introduction, in her exploration of what it means to be a saint, she offers us the definition of literalism: in other words, saints are literalists.[22] For all their faults, one thing that a saint is, in the classical sense of the word, is someone who takes the gospel seriously – even literally. Jesus says to the rich young man, 'sell up and give all your possessions to the poor', so St Francis takes him at his word and presents himself naked in the town square. Jesus says 'love your enemies', and so Etty Hillesum attempts to love the Nazi camp officers as human beings, with families and real emotions. This is the very essence of sainthood, and the very essence of radical discipleship. And whilst it seems unrealistic to expect the rest of the church to follow suit, what these saints do, argues McGinley, is rebuke us in our moderation.

Referring to the radicality of the gospel McGinley notes that these are

> soul-stirring slogans which most of us absent-mindedly attend to and admire as we admire all lofty phrases. We even try to follow them in moderation. We agree that charity covers a multitude of sins and besides is deductable on the Income Tax. We comfort the afflicted in committee or subscribe to a fund for the relief of earthquake victims a hemisphere away. We take flowers to the hospitals, speak with friendship to the folk next door, and give away our old clothes to the deprived.
>
> But the saints, I repeat, are not moderate.[23]

The saints go beyond tax-efficient giving, beyond hand-me-down charity, beyond mere neighbourliness, and like my friend Louis Spence, offer a kind of hospitality that can only be explained by the existence of Jesus and the power of his call. A Rastafarian from Trinidad, Louis converted whilst we were students at university, and very soon was a provocation to the rest of the Christian community. Whereas many of us had already found ways of rationalising the words of Jesus in order to circumvent some of his more radical commands, Louis didn't do that at all – nor does he do so now. Instead he took the words of Jesus literally. So one day when our invited guests failed to show up for a meal that we had prepared at our student house, Louis threatened to take the bowl of stew and go out into the highways and byways of Durham city to see if there was anyone who would like to come instead.

'After all, didn't Jesus say something to that effect?' asked Louis to his incredulous housemates. 'Well, in so many words,' someone muttered. 'But it was only hyperbole,' said another. But as far as Louis was concerned that was just a whole load of spiritual clap-trap – a convenient way for young middle-class aspiring intellectuals to avoid the messiness of ministry to the masses. And just to prove it, he actually went out of the door. In fact he spent the next couple of years going out of the door. His ministry of rounding up waifs and strays was legendary. At one point, we had half of Winterton Mental Health Hospital staying over at our place. On another occasion we had thirteen round our table for Sunday lunch, made up of two families from one of the most notorious housing estates in Durham. And whilst at the time I wondered about the wisdom of having so many people in our house (we learnt the hard way), and whilst I am sure our studies suffered as a result, I will never forget the experience for as long as I live. What Louis taught me and what I hope we will not forget in our churches is that we never get so advanced, so refined in our manners, that we fail to share our table with the stranger. It may sound very basic, and not at all sexy, but it is what lies at the heart of things. Primitive piety begins in worship: at the place of our utter wretchedness. It moves on into transformation: the recovery of our full humanity. It implies the existence of a community as the breeding ground for such transformation. But finally it thrusts out into the world, because as John Chrysostom once preached: 'it is not possible for one to be wealthy and just at the same time.' In other words, we must forsake our comforts and attend to the needs of the world. Indeed, in somewhat graphic language, Chrysostom went on in the next sentence to exclaim his astonishment that the rich could honour their excrements 'as to receive them in a silver chamber pot when another man made in the image of God is perishing in the cold.'[24] Such was his antipathy towards social elitism. For the readers of *Guildford Magazine* this kind of rhetoric might sound offensive. It doesn't go down too well with coffee and croissants. Nevertheless, for all the offence, it is what makes us authentically Christian. Real Christianity of the kind that transforms communities occurs when those who have received the medicine of the gospel end up dispensing it for others.

Conclusion: Holy the Wild

The mistake she made wasn't to fight dirt, sure enough, but to try and do away with it altogether. As if that were possible. A parish is *bound* to be dirty. A whole Christian society's a lot dirtier. You wait for the judgement day and see what the angels'll be sweeping out of even the most saintly monasteries. Some filth! Which all goes to prove, boy, that the Church must needs be a sound housewife – sound and sensible. My nun wasn't a real housewife; a real housewife knows her home isn't a shrine. Those are just poet's dreams.

Georges Bernanos, *The Diary of a Country Priest*

My Christian conversion was a great shock to my mother. Overnight, she had a raving fundamentalist in her home, living out a kind of teenage rebellion, only without the drugs, sex and rock 'n' roll. And given my somewhat self-righteous attitude, she took great delight in catching me out. If I lost my temper, for instance, or spoke unkindly, she would be quick to point out my failure, jibing in the process: 'I thought you were supposed to be a Christian?'

My initial response to this irritation was to try to justify myself. I too was baffled as to why I was still sinning. But after months of doing this it occurred to me that I was adopting the wrong response. After all, what was the point of becoming a Christian, if I was already so holy? The perfection I was striving for did not require a cross. And so instead of defending myself, one day I turned to my mother, following another one of her jibes, and simply said: 'But that is why I am a Christian! It is precisely because

I am not perfect that I have become a Christian.' She never raised the subject again.

Looking back, I have a great deal of sympathy for my mother. It must have been a very frightening experience to suddenly have an evangelical hothead for a son. I admit now that some of my attitudes were less than charitable (and she was a fantastic mum). On the other hand, when she and I reflected in later years on what it was that lay behind her own perceptions of Christian piety, we concluded that it was a vision of holiness that had more to do with middle-class sensibilities than with Christian discipleship. Where she acquired it from, I am not sure. I reckon it to be a strange concoction of English suburban politeness mixed with a tinge of that religious perfectionism so deeply engrained in the Welsh chapel culture of her youth – a lethal combination if ever there was one. And for years I bought into it. Not only her version of it – that was the least of it – but the version that was being pushed from conference podiums and church pulpits across the country.

It is this conformity that I want to challenge in this concluding chapter, not because I have ceased to believe in the moral vision of the Bible – you will find me most conservative on matters of dogma and ethics – but because I have become convinced that we have confused holiness with what I call evangelical correctness. In the process we have made the way of Jesus about as nervous an adventure as it could possibly be. Tied up in the straitjacket of evangelical piety, my observation as a pastor of such a community is that vast tracts of emotional life remain unexplored and unaccounted for. Fearful of putting a foot out of line, we have ceased to reckon on the graciousness by which God takes the idiosyncrasies and inconsistencies of our lives as the stuff of holiness, thus leaving our Christian faith as less a journey into God than an exercise in playing safe. As Dave Hansen puts it: 'Rules kill. Overreligion packs the soul so tight there is no room for the Spirit of God, for the freedom requisite to responsibility, for space that permits light, shadow, inquiry and beauty. Rules and regulations pollute a soul the way silt pollutes a river. It asphyxiates spirit. Tightly packed overreligion is what Jesus fought the Pharisees over. It's what hung him on a cross.'[1]

Real and Actual Lives

This conflict between overreligion and 'space that permits light, shadow, inquiry and beauty,' came to a head for me one Sunday when I was confronted at the end of the service by a very attractive woman with a young daughter in tow, who asked if she could join our church – she and her partner! Clearly the way I replied must have betrayed my concern about her use of the term 'partner', because the next thing she said, practically pinning me against the wall, was, 'So, you don't accept people like me?'

My way of escape, out of what was potentially an embarrassing situation, was to suggest – somewhat cowardly I admit – that we met up later in the week, thus buying me time to think through my response. By Wednesday of that week I felt sufficiently ready for the second round of the contest. Minutes before the bell rang, however, I had this very strong sense that what I needed to do was simply to listen to this woman's story. Pastors listen all the time, of course. Ours is a listening profession. But often our listening is with a view to finding a gap in the narrative: to try out next week's sermon, or to project some of our own problems. It is not listening at all. So what I mean here is *really* listen. Listen not just to her story, which is something I am used to doing, but listen to the ache that wrapped itself around the narrative – and, above all, to suspend judgement.

This I did. At the end of the hour or so of listening to her story – an all too familiar and yet utterly unique story of betrayal – I was left with one unassailable piece of data: that if Jesus had not come into this woman's life, at the point of her utter despair, she would have been dead long ago, either through something like an overdose or throwing herself under a train. Unlike some Christians for whom faith is no more than a lifestyle choice, knowing Christ for this woman was simply a matter of life or death. Moreover, whilst I may have something to say about her living arrangements, and whilst eventually we did get to talk about why she felt so nervous about commitment, at that point in time what she needed was not a whole load of 'oughts' and 'shoulds', but someone who would listen to her story and discern within it – however messy it might appear – the fingerprints of God.

I say this because there are no ideal lives. Even in the Bible there are no ideal lives. The Bible is not a hagiography of the lives of the great saints. Almost every one of the characters in the Bible is ambiguous to say the least. I don't mean to imply by this that anything goes, but rather that some of our versions of Christian piety simply do not do justice to the dramatic contours of the lives of God's people. In fact, the obsession with evangelical correctness means that many of the Bible's narratives flatten, by the time they reach our commentaries, into dead platitudes, leaving the reader with little hope of imagining a Christ-formed life in the vagaries of their own existence. How many commentaries on the life of David, for instance, present him as some kind of Scottish Divine? Reading these pious devotionals one would think David had it all together. Yet here is a man who is as unpredictable as the sea, whose life does not conform to nice neat patterns, but instead is a tapestry of triumph and tragedy. Indeed, the tragedy is as critical as the triumph. The failures in David's life are as spiritually forming as the successes, and oftentimes more necessary. You wouldn't think so reading the average Christian biography. What you get there is the life of the saint with the bad bits excised. Certain publishers of, shall we say, a more Reformed theological persuasion leave you with the impression that their chosen subject is one stop short of full divinity: they never swore, were never tempted, and spent most of their time on their knees in prayer (living proof that Wesley was right after all, and that there is such a thing as sinless perfection). Though some people are utterly inspired by this kind of book, for me such books are utterly useless.

First, they are dishonest. With all respect to my puritan forebears, I don't know anyone like they describe, living or dead. Elijah was a righteous man, so the Bible tells us, but since he was also described as a man just like us, it forces us to redefine what we mean by righteousness. Does it mean unflappable? Having an answer for every question? If it does then Elijah is an odd example. One minute we find him riding high on a glorious moment of prophetic victory at Mount Carmel; the next minute running for his life and wishing he was dead – all in a *couple* of chapters.[2] Or consider Abraham. Here he is one minute, leaving home for a country whose architect and builder is God; the next minute he is selling his wife into an Egyptian harem to save his own skin – all within *one* chapter.[3]

These mood swings of the great heroes of the faith, even fathers of the faith, ought to allay our fears concerning our own humanity. If someone like Elijah was prone to bouts of depression, then it ought to come as no surprise when we are too. As Michael Plekon puts it, in his examination of sainthood within his own Orthodox tradition:

> Holiness, further, does not require the absence of sin and human qualities, eccentricities, phobias, sufferings – the substance of ordinary life. Holiness is a struggle with the baggage of human existence, all the elements that make us who we are. Despite the claims of hagiography, the written lives of the saints, and the characteristics deemed necessary for official church recognition or canonisation, the personalities and lives of the saints remain truly human and particular, even imperfect.[4]

As long as we conceive piety along the lines of more sanguine temperaments, then the richness of such imperfect lives will remain largely unexplored, with the more melancholic, depressive types condemned to the margins of Christian spirituality.

I know this to be partly true, because I myself am on the melancholic end of the personality spectrum – verging on slightly manic tendencies, so my friends tell me. But whereas in certain circles this state might be celebrated as artistic genius,[5] the erratic behaviour that inevitably accompanies such a personality is often frowned upon within the Christian community. It is condescendingly viewed as something less than holy, for to be holy is to be balanced: 'Be balanced for I am balanced,' says the Lord. In fact, it seems to me that there has been something of a conspiracy in the Christian world over the past few decades to ensure that all the songs, and all the sermons, and even all the prayers, support this kind of equanimity. This is great if you happen to fall into that category, or if you are experiencing life like that. But it is disastrous if you are not, because it effectively shuts down whole octaves of human emotions as 'out of bounds' for the Christian.

It is an interesting situation to find ourselves in. Why do we assume that when God is on the move in a person's life it will, by definition, result in a balanced life? Abraham wasn't balanced.[6] Anyone who takes his son up a mountain with a knife in hand, intent – right up to the eleventh hour – to slay him, is hardly balanced; nor is someone who weeps at the feet of Jesus, wiping her tears with her long, luscious and loose hair.[7] That is an act more aptly described as erotic than it is balanced, and one likely to get you thrown out of decent society. In fact, when you consider it, one is hard pressed to recall any balanced personality in the Bible at all. I do not mean to make a virtue out of eccentricity, but simply to say that our modern predilection for pain-free, emotionally-balanced living is somewhat alien to the Bible. What we find there is a God who seems to delight in whole octaves of emotions, from the rawest anger to the laughter. As Barth so playfully put it:

> The heroes in the Bible are to a certain degree quite respectable, but to serve as examples to the good, efficient, industrious, publicly educated, average citizen of Switzerland, men like Samson, David, Amos, and Peter are very ill-fitted indeed. Rosa of Tannenburg, the figures of Amicus' 'Courage' (Il Cuore), and the magnificent characters of later Swiss history are quite different people. The Bible is an embarrassment in the school and foreign to it.[8]

Over-realised Hope

Part of the problem is the way we read the New Testament: reading it retrospectively from the vantage point of the end, and fostering, as a result, a kind of smugness that every question has already found its resolution. Or, more specifically, reading the New Testament, like the Corinthians did, as if the resurrection of Christ has already projected us into a world where struggle and pain are no more.

It is an easy error to make. We can hardly read the New Testament any other way but retrospectively. We live post-resurrection. And given the scale of what happened that first Easter Sunday, it is no surprise that our faith spills over into triumphalism. But as Paul points out in both his epistles to the

Corinthians – who were especially guilty of an over-realised version of the victory of God – a Christianity that focuses entirely on the resurrection, or makes resurrection synonymous with the success culture of the world around us, is one that fails to take account of the very real journey of endurance that still exists for the Christian living between the times – between the 'now' of the resurrection but the 'not yet' of its consummation. Furthermore, it is a Christianity that fails to take account of its very real purpose in the process of spiritual formation. For it is only in suffering, as all the New Testament writers attest to, that deep faith is forged. If we insist on bypassing suffering by resort to a gospel of pleasant optimism, then all we will have is an attenuated faith: happy songs, for happy people, for an oh-so-happy God. We will never discover the depths of a faith hammered out on the anvil of pain. Vast tracts of our emotional terrain will be left unexplored.

Of course, there is an equal and opposite danger here. When my friends hear me talk this way, they warn me that I am getting too morbid, and committing an error in the opposite direction by making a virtue out of suffering. It is a charge I accept to some degree. As someone who actually likes tragedies, and reads Thomas Hardy for fun, I admit that is a possibility. In fact, so aware am I of the danger that a few years ago a number of us recovering melancholics conceived the idea of a new club called Melancholics Anonymous, the first step of our 12 step recovery programme being: 'We are powerless to do anything about our love of tragedy.'

However, even though there is a danger here of confusing suffering with morbidity and minimising, furthermore, the crushing and destructive effects of depression, nevertheless it is the tragic element, as Forsyth pointed out, that uncovers for us the true contours of a mature faith. Grace, as we have said before, can only be truly celebrated against the backcloth of judgement; praise can only really mature in those who have known the depths of lament; the 'wings of the dove' the Psalmist sings about can only really be appreciated by those who have known the 'pits' of despair.[9] As American poet Mary Oliver puts it in her poem, 'A Certain Sharpness in the Morning Air':

for it is true isn't it,
in our world,
that the petals pooled with nectar, and the polished thorns
are a single thing –
that even the purest light, lacking the robe of darkness,
would be without expression –
that love itself, without its pain, would be
no more than a shruggable comfort.[10]

Without the thorns, worship ends up as no more than a 'shruggable comfort'; without the angst that accompanies the tragic element, faith lacks real drama and is flattened out to platitudinous sayings; without that sense of danger that lies at the heart of Israel's faith – often lacking because we presume it to be resolved by the time we get to the New Testament – our gatherings degenerate into all the right words, but not interior knowledge as to why these things are critical for our lives. As Isaiah puts it: 'These people honour me with their lips, but their hearts are far from me.'[11] Faith ceases to be an adventure of the soul, but attenuates into pious sentimentality, or moralistic behaviour.

A New Vision of Holiness

How we begin to transform contemporary models of holiness is not entirely clear. The challenges are formidable. Conservative evangelicalism with its penchant for theological correctness sees mess as a compromise, whereas radical evangelicalism, with its own penchant for glory, sees mess as failure. The legalistic tendencies of both traditions stifle true spiritual growth by suggesting that holiness is linear.

The movements of the soul, however, never conform to neat, predictable patterns. Instead, they operate like the soil of the earth: that organic beauty of something that is both responsive and yet vulnerable. In other words, holiness is not striving for some illusory perfection, but rather an exercise in heartfelt loyalty in which we daily invite the Holy Spirit to work the earth of the heart. It is not so much a scheme, as some models of discipleship suggest, nor a particular teaching, although it must include that, of course, but a mystical union. Primitive piety in no way reneges on the morality of holiness but defines it in such a way that it stretches the possibilities of what we might include within that holiness, especially what we might call the fire of passion.[12] Devoid of a burning bush, Israel's escapades in Egypt are nothing more than a political agenda. Stripped of the beauty of holiness, Christian piety is nothing more than middle-class niceness – just about the worst expression of Christian piety one could imagine. But place fire at the centre and then you have a faith that is elemental.

If it is the case that holiness is more than simply religious behaviour, then it seems to me that the heart of what God requires of us is humility. Above and beyond our formulas on holy living, or our schemes for sanctification, is the simple and basic instinct to keep our hearts open before the God who has rescued us. Holiness is not meant to be analysed. The person who keeps checking their spiritual temperature is a perfectionist.[13] Rather, the holy life is a life lived for God in its entirety: the whole of us before the whole of God. At times this will require us to be incredibly scrupulous; at other times to be relaxed. Both postures are important. The trick, it seems, is to know when to be which. Sometimes we are relaxed with ourselves when we ought to be tough; other times we are hard on ourselves when we ought to be soft. And the consequences of getting it wrong can be devastating. One leads to legalism, the other to licentiousness. If we are to be truly Christian we must reckon on faith working through love. But underlying it all, and common to both, is recognition of utter dependency. As David puts it, as he wrestles with his own inconsistencies, 'You do not delight in sacrifice or I would bring it; you do not take pleasure in burnt offerings. The sacrifices of God are a broken spirit; a broken and a contrite heart, O God, you will not despise.'[14] God is not impressed by our self-flagellation, just as he is not pleased by our indifference. Both are worthless to him. What he delights in is a heart that is exposed to him: soil that is willing to be turned over for God to plant fresh seeds of his word; that is humble enough and broken enough to yield itself to the fresh workings of the Holy Spirit. When the writer to the Hebrews exhorts his congregation to the way of holiness he does not throw the rule book at him – at least not in the first instance.

Paraenesis comes right at the end of the letter, and often by way of reminder. More important for our preacher is the urgency for the congregation to be open to the living and immediate word of God. Quoting Psalm 95, the preacher exhorts the congregation that 'today, if you hear his voice, do not harden your hearts.'[15]

Vital Christianity always has this presentness about it; and either we yield to the vitality of it, or we harden. There is no neutral ground. Such is the intensity of the life of faith that each day places us in the valley of decision. At times this voice will be hard. The word has that ability to penetrate the inveterate deceptiveness of the human heart. It can divide 'soul and spirit, joints and marrow; it judges the thoughts and attitudes of the heart.' There is no place where we can hide. 'Nothing in all creation is hidden from God's sight. Everything is uncovered and laid bare before the eyes of him to whom we must give an account.'[16] If we think that by following God we have signed up for a life of ease, we are badly mistaken and poorly advised. The word is like a hammer. It will be like that until the end. But at least we can comfort ourselves with the fact that we are still hearing it. It's when we don't hear God's word that we should worry. For it will be a sign that we have given up on the project of a transformed humanity.

Coming from the Reformed tradition as I do, I admit to feeling somewhat nervous about what I have proposed. There seems little respite in what I have proposed from the relentlessness of God's working the earth of the heart, and hardly any bulwark against the threat of judgement. But maybe this is what the Reformers understood by assurance. In other words, the doctrine of assurance was not some anodyne teaching designed to put us to sleep. Rather, it portrays that precarious state of existence where we live daily between the ever-present deservedness of judgement and the ever-present gift of grace; where we live suspended on the possibility of utter annihilation but also the infinitude of divine care. As Luther observes in his commentary on Psalm 130: 'Whoever, therefore, does not consider the judgement of God, does not fear; and whoever does not fear, does not cry out, and whoever does not cry out, finds no grace.'[17]

Whether suburban Christianity can bear such intensity is unlikely. As Eliot wrote, 'humankind/Cannot bear very much reality.' He meant not that humankind cannot bear the reality of the world, but cannot bear the ultimate Reality: of God, prayer, the logos, mercy, judgement.[18] Hence our piety tends towards a kind of moralism and, as a consequence, an inevitable propensity to justify ourselves at the expense of others. What the psalmist offers us instead, as Brian Brock has shown, is a much more dramatic, as well as interesting narrative, whereby prayer, worship and the presence of God leads us ever onwards into an awareness of our sins and the gift of repentance: 'Without God's constant forgiveness, we do not see our own sin; and without the exposure of our sins and our repenting of them, we remain in the deadening byways down which other gods have enticed us.'[19] Without grace we become like the Pharisee in Luke 18. Impervious to the mercies of God, convinced of our own righteousness, we end up trapped in a world of our own making – a paradoxically mediocre one. On the other hand, the sinner in the parable goes away from the scene justified, because the hallmark of true piety is not the absence of struggle, a settled smugness about where one has got to, but precisely the opposite: the immediacy of a life of prayer whereby every morning we confess that but for the Lord's mercies we would be utterly consumed. William Countryman offers us much the same vision of holiness in one of his poems:

> Your choice of friends is broad
> And (may we say?) unpredictable.
> What did you see in Jacob?
> Esau was bluff, hearty,
> a man's man – overconfident,
> to be sure – even a minute
> or two of seniority can grant
> a certain status. Jacob's
> only accomplishments were to cheat
> his brother (with Esau's rash
> cooperation yes) and deceive
> his father. Piety suggests
> you should have judged the scamp
> and left him to stew in his guilt
> till he repented. Instead,
> you showed him by night the ladder
> to your throne.[20]

And so it is, years on, that I am now presented with a rather different vision of holiness to the one with which I began my journey. It is not a less rigorous one. In some ways it is more intense. But even so, it is a holiness that is arguably more interesting as well as more biblical, for it takes into account the raw stuff of our humanity. A primitive kind of piety means the celebration of every particle of our humanity in the knowledge that it is only this, and not anything else, that God can redeem. Speaking of saints and sinners, Rowan Williams urges us to stop deifying our saints and stop shaming our sinners. In the end, they are much the same thing. An alleluia for saints is not a celebration of perfection but of a life lived wholly before God; conversely, an alleluia for sinners is not an exposé of the most shameful acts, but rather 'an alleluia for people who are able to ask themselves the awkward questions.'[21] My hope is that *Primitive Piety* will have gone some way to asking these awkward questions, offering us a vision of holiness that is wild, and a wildness that is holy.

Epilogue

Luke 7:36–50

[36] When one of the Pharisees invited Jesus to have dinner with him, he went to the Pharisee's house and reclined at the table. [37] A woman in that town who lived a sinful life learned that Jesus was eating at the Pharisee's house, so she came there with an alabaster jar of perfume. [38] As she stood behind him at his feet weeping, she began to wet his feet with her tears. Then she wiped them with her hair, kissed them and poured perfume on them.
[39] When the Pharisee who had invited him saw this, he said to himself, 'If this man were a prophet, he would know who is touching him and what kind of woman she is – that she is a sinner.'
[40] Jesus answered him, 'Simon, I have something to tell you.'
'Tell me, teacher,' he said.
[41] 'Two people owed money to a certain moneylender. One owed him five hundred denarii, and the other fifty. [42] Neither of them had the money to pay him back, so he forgave the debts of both. Now which of them will love him more?'
[43] Simon replied, 'I suppose the one who had the bigger debt forgiven.'
'You have judged correctly,' Jesus said.
[44] Then he turned toward the woman and said to Simon, 'Do you see this woman? I came into your house. You did not give me any water for my feet, but she wet my feet with her tears and wiped them with her hair. [45] You did not give me a kiss, but this woman, from the time I entered, has not stopped kissing my feet. [46] You did not put oil on my head, but she has poured perfume on my

feet. [47] Therefore, I tell you, her many sins have been forgiven – as her great love has shown. But whoever has been forgiven little loves little.'

[48] Then Jesus said to her, 'Your sins are forgiven.'

[49] The other guests began to say among themselves, 'Who is this who even forgives sins?'

[50] Jesus said to the woman, 'Your faith has saved you; go in peace.'

Luke 7:36–50 is memorable for me for being the only passage I have preached twice in the same place. And according to the one person who remembered the first occasion, apparently it was better the second time round.

That aside, it is Kenneth Bailey in his outstanding cultural reading of the parables in Luke who points out the sexual overtones of this scene.[1] Not only is the woman in the scene carrying a perfumed sachet between her breasts, like any common prostitute, but her hair is loose – a state of appearance more befitting for the bedroom than for a Bible study. Indeed, it is the use of her long tresses to dry the feet of Jesus with her tears that breaks the camel's back for Simon, who now condemns her for overtly touching the teacher – and accuses Jesus of sheer naivety.

As with many of the gospel stories, we have lived with this episode for so long that the rawness of the encounter has become dulled. We need a good exegete to roughen the text a little, and remind us how explicit all this is. It is one of those occasions when sexuality and spirituality sit dangerously close to one another. It would be so easy for us to sanitise the scene, and claim less for the woman than is actually happening. After all, this is worship, not seduction. At no point does Jesus receive her attentions as anything other than spiritual devotion. Yet, for all the devotion, it is sensual at the same time – unmistakably physical. This is not reasonable worship, to quote the *King James Version*, but rather the offering of our bodies in something altogether more extreme, irrational even.

And whilst it makes Simon uncomfortable, it seems not to trouble Jesus in the slightest. On the contrary, he welcomes it, or, more to the point, welcomes her, not because there is a virtue in exuberance *per se* – it would be a mistake to preach this text in order to cajole this kind of thing – but simply because this is what real faith looks like. It cannot be any other way. If there is any logic at work in the story it is not the logic of Simon, who clearly has only invited Jesus to test his credentials as a prophet, but the logic of her response. As Jesus says, she loved much because she was forgiven much.[2] In other words, the exuberance of her love was proportionate to the forgiveness she had been shown. That we love little is a reflection of our failure to understand our sin. That we love much is because we have experienced firsthand the breathless gratitude of the despairing soul. As Paul Tillich reminds us, 'We cannot love unless we have accepted forgiveness, and the deeper our experience of forgiveness is, the greater is our love.'[3]

For sure, the exuberance of the love is unconventional. It's a wonder she was not thrown out of the room. Only her proximity to Jesus prevents this happening. But in another way it is not the woman's exuberance that is unconventional but Simon's inhospitality. He has omitted to give even the most basic of greetings. Had he done so – had he kissed his guest on arrival, had he washed his feet, had he anointed him with oil – it is possible this scene would never have transpired. But what is clear is that his shock over such lavish expressions of love is only because she exaggerates what he had largely forgotten or neglected. That he was offended was not because the woman had transgressed, but because he had not transgressed enough. He did not know what it was like to feel forgiveness in the guts. She at least has sins worth forgiving: real sins that need a real saviour. Our debts, or at least our perception of them, are barely enough to muster a priest, let alone a saviour.

To a heart that is shrivelled, like Simon's – who has no internal instinct as to the crisis in his own soul – the sight of a woman fawning over the feet of Jesus will always seem odd. How else was he supposed to see it? If you had lived your life like Simon's, staying clear of those liminal spaces in life, doing all things well, living ever so conservatively, you too would see it that way; nothing more than a woman unhinged. But Jesus knows differently: that the dangerous yet unashamed mixture of tears, allure, and loose hair, pouring over his feet, is precisely what happens when the mystery of the word is performed. And so it is, not for the first time in scripture, that a woman rebukes us for our lack of realism.

Like Tamar of old, or Rahab, Ruth, Deborah, Hannah and Abigail, the sheer honesty of this unnamed woman's piety acts as a foil for the hypocrisy of so many of our male responses. If we think that tears are a sign of weakness, something that big boys should not indulge in, it is Luke's intention to show us through this woman that instead they are a sign of life.

Primitive piety is not some macho, warrior-like faith that refuses to weep; any more than it is an exclusively feminine thing where we get in touch with our emotions. That would reduce faith to gender stereotypes. But even so, it takes a woman, a beaten-down woman at that, to remind us that real faith is forged more often than not *in extremis*. It is joyful precisely because it has learned to weep. It weeps in the night precisely because joy has come in the morning. Encounter with Jesus doesn't flatten our personality; that is the preserve of sin. Instead, it takes personality to new heights. Holiness is wild even as it is reverent.

Endnotes

Preface

[1] R. Alter, *The Art of Biblical Poetry*, New York: Basic Books, 2011, 140–141.

Introduction

[1] Quoted in D. Johnson, *The Glory of Preaching: Participating in God's Transformation of the World*, Downers Grove: IVP, 2009, 62. Homiletically, Johnson's point is that so much that passes for preaching is not the indicative of the gospel, but the imperatives of good behaviour.

[2] For an expose of Christian niceness, see P. Couglin, *No More Christian Nice Guy*, Minneapolis: Bethany Books, 2005.

[3] P. McGinley, *Saint Watching*, London: Collins, 1970, 19.

[4] Quoted in H. Barrett and J. Phillips, *Suburban Style: The British Home, 1840–1960*, London: Macdonald Orbis, 1988, 11.

[5] P.T. Forsyth, *Positive Preaching and the Modern Mind*, London: Independent Press, 1964 [1907], 244.

[6] C. Binfield, 'P.T. Forsyth as Congregational Minister,' in T. Hart ed. *Justice, The True and Only Mercy: Essays on the Life and Theology of Peter Taylor Forsyth*, Edinburgh: T&T Clark, 1995, 21.

[7] D.L. Goetz, *Death by Suburb: How to Keep the Suburbs from Killing Your Soul*, New York: Harper One, 2006, 9.

[8] J. Updike, *Run Rabbit Run*, New York: Alfred A. Knopf, 1970, 237.

[9] J. Clemo, *Selected Poems*, Newcastle Upon Tyne: Bloodaxe Books, 1988, 62–63.

[10] D. Sayers, *The Whimsical Christian: 18 Essays by Dorothy Sayers*, New York: Macmillan, 1987, 27.

[11] B. Thomson, *Gauguin's Vision*, Edinburgh: National Galleries of Scotland, 2005, 39.

[12] W. Blacker, *Along the Enchanted Way: A Romanian Story*, London: John Murray, 2009, 37.

[13] W. Kilpatrick, *Psychological Seduction: The Failure of Modern Psychology*, London: Arthur James Limited, 1983, 138.

[14] M. Plekon, *Hidden Holiness*, Indiana: Notre Dame, 2009, 39.

[15] Quoted in D.W. Fagerberg, 'The Essential Chesterton', in *First Things*, March 2000, 23–26.

[16] Taken from the Foreword of P. Woodhouse, *Etty Hillesum: A Life Transformed*, London: Continuum, 2009.

[17] See McGinley, *Saint Watching*, 22.

[18] In an interview, Yates detailed the title's subtext: 'I think I meant it more as an indictment of American life in the 1950s. Because during the Fifties there was a general lust for conformity all over this country, by no means only in the suburbs – a kind of blind, desperate clinging to safety and security at any price, as exemplified politically in the Eisenhower administration and the Joe McCarthy witch-hunts. Anyway, a great many Americans were deeply disturbed by all that – felt it to be an outright betrayal of our best and bravest revolutionary spirit – and that was the spirit I tried to embody in the character of April Wheeler. I meant the title to suggest that the revolutionary road of 1776 has come to something very much like a dead end in the Fifties.' Henry DeWitt and Geoffrey Clark, 'An Interview with Richard Yates', *Ploughshares*, Winter 1972.

[19] M. Bunting, *The Plot: A Biography of an English Acre*, London: Granta Books, 2009.

[20] Forsyth, *Positive Preaching*, 244.

[21] E.M. Humphrey, *Grand Entrance: Worship on Earth as in Heaven*, Grand Rapids: Brazos Press, 2011, 3.

[22] Matthew 10:34.

[23] J. Osborne, *Look Back in Anger*, London: Faber & Faber, 1996 [1957], 100.

Chapter One – Holy Love

1. J. Moltmann, *The Crucified God*, New York: Harper and Row, 1974, 108.

2. J.B. Green and M.D. Baker, *Recovering the Scandal of the Cross: Atonement in New Testament and Contemporary Contexts*, Downers Grove: IVP, 2000, 116–152.

3. P.T. Forsyth, *The Cruciality of the Cross*, Rochester: Stanhope Press, 1948, 39.

4. See L. McCurdy, *Attributes and Atonement: The Holy Love of God in the Theology of P.T. Forsyth*, Milton Keynes: Paternoster, 1999.

5. F. Buechner, *Wishful Thinking: A Theological ABC*, San Francisco: Harper, 1993, 91.

6. 2 Corinthians 5:21.

7. K. Menninger, *Whatever Became of Sin?*, New York: Hawthorn Books, 1973.

8. See Kilpatrick, *Psychological Seduction*, for a restatement of the classical doctrine of sin over against the cult of the therapeutic.

9. E.H. Peterson, *Five Smooth Stones for Pastoral Work*, Grand Rapids/Leominster: Eerdmans/Gracewing, 1992 [1980], 138.

10. F. Dostoevsky, *The Idiot*, translated by Alan Myers, Oxford: OUP, 1992, 159.

11. K. Norris, *Amazing Grace: The Vocabulary of Grace*, New York: Riverhead Books, 1998, 165.

12. Forsyth, *Positive Preaching*, 244.

13. Ibid., 244.

14. Kilpatrick, *Psychological Seduction*, 95.

15. Forsyth, *The Cruciality of the Cross*, 30.

16. Ibid., 31.

17. Forsyth, *Positive Preaching*, 124.

18. H. Urs von Balthasar, *Prayer*, San Francisco: Ignatius Press, 1986 [1955], 224.

19. D. Bonhoeffer, *Meditations on the Cross* (ed. M. Weber), Louisville: John Knox Press, 1996, 71.

20. See R. Mouw, *The Smell of Sawdust: What Evangelicals Can Learn from their Fundamentalist Heritage*, Grand Rapids: Zondervan, 2000.

21. D. Hansen, *The Art of Pastoring: Ministry Without All the Answers*, Downers Grove: IVP, 1994, 84.

22. Sayers, *The Whimsical Christian*, 27.

23 I am contrasting two books here: *Love Wins* (London: Collins, 2011), by Rob Bell, which stirred up a great deal of controversy for its unabashed universalism, and *God Wins: Heaven, Hell and Why the Good News is Better than Love Wins*, Carol Stream: Tyndale House Publishers, 2011, which is Mark Galli's response to the debate.

24 T. Eagleton, *Reason, Faith, and Revolution: Reflections on the God Debate*, New Haven/London: Yale University Press, 2010, 168–169.

25 R. Guardini, *The Lord*, Washington: Regnery/Gateway, 1982 [1954], 532.

Chapter Two – Undiscovered Octaves

1 W. Brueggemann, *The Psalms and the Life of Faith*, Minneapolis: Fortress Press, 1995, 15.

2 Exodus 32:18.

3 J. Durham, *Exodus*, Waco: Word Biblical Commentaries, 1987, 424.

4 P. Greenslade, *Worship in the Best of Both Worlds: Explorations in Ancient-Future Worship*, Milton Keynes: Paternoster, 2009, xiv.

5 M. Dawn, *A Royal Waste of Time: The Splendor of Worshipping God and Being Church for the World*, Grand Rapids: Eerdmans, 1999, 7.

6 A. Dillard, *Teaching a Stone to Talk*, New York: Harper Collins, 1982, 58–59.

7 See S.T. Kimbrough, Jr, ed., *Orthodox and Wesleyan Spirituality*, Crestwood: St Vladimir's Press, 2002.

8 B. Brown Taylor, *Leaving Church: A Memoir of Faith*, Harper: San Francisco, 2006, 147–148.

9 Ibid., 148.

10 N. Wolterstorff, *Lament for a Son*, London: Spire, 1989, 86.

11 E.H. Peterson, *Christ Plays in Ten Thousand Places: A Conversation in Spiritual Theology*, London: Hodder and Stoughton, 2005, 41–42.

12 R. Otto, *The Idea of the Holy*, transl. J.W. Harvey, Oxford: Oxford University Press, 1958 [1923].

13 Ephesians 4:30.

14 Hebrews 12:18–29.

15 K. Grahame, *The Wind in the Willows*, London: Methuen Children's Books, 1971, 139.

16 'Worship the Lord in the Beauty of Holiness' in *The Baptist Hymn Book*, London: Psalms and Hymns Trust, 1971, Hymn 35.

Chapter Three – Honest Prayer

[1] S. Hauerwas, *Prayers Plainly Spoken*, London: Triangle, 1999, 26.

[2] Ibid., 64.

[3] S. Hauerwas, *Hannah's Child: A Theologian's Memoir*, London: SCM Press, 2010, 256.

[4] E.H. Peterson, *Answering God: The Psalms as Tools for Prayer*, San Francisco: Harper & Row, 1989, 37.

[5] I am grateful to Graham Cray for this insight. In Romans 8:26ff, the groanings of prayer, which possibly refer to tongues, are reflected in two other groanings in the passage: the groaning of creation, longing to be freed from its bondage to decay, and the groanings of the Spirit. In other words, our groaning pitches in between the groaning of God and the world.

[6] Genesis 34:22–32.

[7] Luke 18:1–8.

[8] Luke 11:5–8.

[9] Colossians 4:12.

[10] Luke 22:44.

[11] D. Hansen, *Long Wandering Prayer*, Oxford: The Bible Reading Fellowship, 2002, 95.

[12] See my chapter 'Confession and Complaint: Christian Pastoral Reflections on Lamentations', in *Great is thy Faithfulness?: Reading Lamentations as Sacred Scripture*, Eugene: Wipf and Stock, 2011, 198–209.

[13] Lamentations 1:12.

[14] Lamentations 2:20.

[15] Lamentations 5:20.

[16] Psalm 55:7

[17] D. Thomas, *The Love Letters of Dylan Thomas*, London: Phoenix, 2001, 8.

[18] See W. Brueggemann, *Spirituality of the Psalms*, Minneapolis: Fortress, 2002, who describes three distinct features in the Psalms: phases of orientation, disorientation, and reorientation. It is important to note that reorientation, for Brueggemann, is not a return to settled existence, but a moving forward to a new place, carrying with it the things we learnt when our world was turned upside down.

[19] Mark 15:34–35.

[20] S.J. Land, *Pentecostal Spirituality: A Passion for the Kingdom*, Sheffield: Sheffield Academic Press, 1994, 44.

21 1 Samuel 1:9–17.

22 J.V. Taylor, *The Christlike God*, London: SCM, 1992, 278.

23 2 Samuel 24:14.

24 Hansen, *Long Wandering Prayer*, 92–93.

25 In fact, extempore prayer is possibly more vulnerable to hackneyed phrases, and therefore less honest, precisely because it lacks liturgical discipline. See P.T. Forsyth on public prayer, *The Soul of Prayer*, Vancouver: Regent Publishing, 2002 [1916], 43.

26 Psalm 137:9.

27 A. Michaels, *Fugitive Pieces*, London: Bloomsbury, 2009, 54.

28 Hansen, *Long Wandering Prayer*, 18–21.

29 1 Peter 5:7.

30 1 Thessalonians 5:17.

31 2 Corinthians 12:8–9.

32 Forsyth, *The Soul of Prayer*, 98.

33 2 Samuel 12:22–23.

34 Forsyth, *The Soul of Prayer*, 107.

35 Luke 11:9–10.

36 Luke 18:6–7.

37 Forsyth, *The Soul of Prayer*, 101–102.

38 Genesis 18:24.

39 Exodus 32:11.

40 Psalm 6:5; c.f. Psalm 30:8–10.

41 Romans 8:26.

42 Romans 8:27.

43 Forsyth, *The Soul of Prayer*, 108.

Chapter Four – In Your Anger Do Not Sin

1 For a further exploration of this theme see I. Stackhouse and O. Crisp (eds), *Text Message*, Eugene: Wipf & Stock, forthcoming.

2 Matthew 5:21–22.

3 Ephesians 4:26–27.

4 A. Trollope, *The Warden*, London: Penguin, 2004, 45.

5 James 1:19–20.

6 Ephesians 4:31.

7 T. Nhat Hanh, *Anger: Buddhist Wisdom for Cooling the Flames*, London: Rider, 2001.

[8] Cited in *What Luther Says: An Anthology*, Vol 1, comp, Ewald. M. Plass, St Louis, Concordia Publishing House, 1959, entry no 74, 27.

[9] Quoted in T. Radcliffe, *What is the Point of Being a Christian?*, London: Continuum, 2005, 80.

[10] J. Wittenberg, *The Silence of Dark Water: An Inner Journey*, London: Robin Clark Limited, 2008, 185.

[11] Matthew 11:28.

[12] 2 Corinthians 10:1.

[13] 1 Thessalonians 2:7.

[14] John 2:14–15.

[15] M. Galli, *Jesus Mean and Wild: The Unexpected Love of an Untameable God*, Grand Rapids: Baker Books, 2008.

[16] 2 Corinthians 13:3–5.

[17] S. Cherry, *Barefoot Disciple: Walking the Way of Passionate Humility*, London: Continuum, 2011, 50–51.

[18] http://www.durhamcathedral.co.uk/schedule/sermons/122.

[19] Matthew 6:14–15.

[20] W. Blake, 'A Poison Tree', in *A Choice of Blake's Verse*, London: Faber and Faber, 1970, 65–66.

[21] Hebrews 12:15.

[22] See D.C. Anderson and P. Mullin (eds), *Faking it: The Sentimentalisation of Modern Society*, London: Penguin, 1998.

[23] K.M. O'Connor, *Lamentations and the Tears of the World*, Maryknoll: Orbis Books, 2002, 87–89.

[24] L. Basset, *Holy Anger: Jacob, Job, Jesus*, London: Continuum, 2007, 80–81.

Chapter Five – Delighting in Our Desires

[1] G. Keillor, *Lake Wobegon Days*, London: Faber and Faber, 1987, 103.

[2] See L. Ryken, *Worldly Saints: The Puritans as They Really Were*, Grand Rapids: Zondervan, 1986.

[3] Jeremiah 17:9.

[4] J. Peters, *Great Revivalists: 1700 to the Present Day*, Farnham: CWR, 2008, 36–37.

[5] Matthew 10:19.

[6] Interestingly, the Welsh claim Hopkins as one of their poets. See G. Morgan (ed.), *This World of Wales: An Anthology of Anglo-Welsh Poetry*, Cardiff: University of Wales Press, 1968, 45–47.

7 R.B. Martin, *Gerard Manley Hopkins: A Very Private Life*, London: Flamingo, 1992, 206–208.

8 G. Manley Hopkins, 'God's Grandeur' in *Gerard Manley Hopkins: Poetry and Prose*, London: Penguin Classics, 1985, 27.

9 See A. Krivak, *A Long Retreat*, London: DLT, 2008.

10 For a helpful discussion of this term in New Testament usage see G. Fee, *Paul, The Spirit and The People of God*, Peabody: Hendrickson Publishers, 1994, 126–139.

11 See O. O'Donovan, *Resurrection and Moral Order: An Outline for Evangelical Ethics*, Leicester: Apollos, 1986, for an exploration of this theme.

12 See P. Sherry, *Spirit and Beauty: An Introduction to Aesthetics*, Oxford: Clarendon, 1992.

13 S. Maitland, *A Book of Silence*, London: Granta, 2008, 189–222.

14 See B.J. Miller-McLemore, *Also a Mother: Work and Family as Theological Dilemma*, Nashville: Abingdon, 1994, for a full exploration of this theme.

15 P. Borgman, *Genesis: The Story We Haven't Heard*, Downers Grove: IVP, 2001, 57–69.

16 G. Lloyd Carr, *The Song of Solomon: The Tyndale Old Testament Commentaries*, Leicester/Downers Grove: IVP, 1984, 26.

17 Quoted in P. Sheldrake, *Befriending our Desires*, London: DLT, 2001, 80.

18 For an assessment of what is perceived in recent years as a more relaxed but not overly wholesome attitude towards sex among evangelicals see R. Clapp, *Tortured Wonders: Christian Spirituality for People, Not Angels*, Grand Rapids: Brazos Press, 2004.

19 C.S. Lewis, *The Weight of Glory and Other Addresses*, Grand Rapids: Eerdmans, 1965, 1–2.

20 A. Ecclestone, *Yes to God*, London: DLT, 1975, 88.

21 R. Alter, *The Book of Psalms: A Translation with Commentary*, W.W. Norton & Company, New York/London, 2007: 297.

22 See C.S. Lewis, *The Four Loves*, London: Geoffrey Bles, 1960.

23 See *Saving Desire: The Seduction of Christian Theology*, F. LeRon Shults and J.O. Hendricksen (eds), Grand Rapids: Eerdmans, 2011, for a thorough theological critique of this classic distinction between agape and eros love.

24 Woodhouse, *Etty Hillesum*, 42.

25 Quoted in R.W. Jenson, *Song of Songs: Interpretation*, Louisville: John Knox, 2005, 18.

[26] J. Donne, 'Sonnet 14', in *The Complete English Poems*, ed. A.J. Smith, London: Penguin Books, 1983, 315.

[27] See J. Stubbs, *Donne: The Reformed Soul*, London: Penguin, 2006, 464–467 for the debate among Donne's biographers at the time concerning these two parts of Donne's personality.

Chapter Six – Surprised by Joy

[1] U. Eco, *The Name of the Rose*, London: Minerva, 1992.

[2] Ibid., 474.

[3] Ibid., 475.

[4] Quoted in the first chapter of Alpha, N. Gumble, *Questions of Life*, Eastbourne: Kingsway, 1993, 11, because Alpha, of course, is itself something of a critique of what it regards as dull, tepid, institutional Christianity. Hence, the first talk in the Alpha series is entitled: 'Christianity: Boring, Untrue and Irrelevant?'

[5] Quoted in E. Peterson, *The Journey: A Guide Book for the Pilgrim Life*, London: Marshall Pickering, 1995, 81.

[6] See D.D. Webster, *A Passion for Christ: An Evangelical Christology*, Grand Rapids: Academie Books, 1987, 79–81, who accuses evangelical Christology, as we noted in the previous chapter, of practical docetism: that is, a christology that fails to take seriously the full humanity of Jesus, and thus promotes an over-worldly, overly pious, kind of spirituality.

[7] P. Morden, 'Spurgeon and Humour', in *The Bible in Transmission: A Forum for Change in Church and Culture*, Swindon: Bible Society, 2011, 20.

[8] See *St Benedict's Rule for Monasteries*, transl. L.J. Doyle, Collegeville: The Liturgical Press, 1935, 27–28.

[9] Genesis 18:12ff. See also Mark 5:35–40.

[10] Luke 6:21.

[11] Luke 6:25.

[12] James 4:9.

[13] P. Berger, *A Rumour of Angels: Modern Society and a Rediscovery of the Supernatural*, London: Penguin, 1969, 89–92. 'By laughing at the imprisonment of the human spirit, humour implies that the imprisonment is not final but will be overcome, and by this implication provides provided yet another signal of transcendence – in this instance

in the form of an intimation of redemption. I would thus argue that humour, like childhood and play, can be seen as an ultimately religious vindication of joy'.

14 J.-J. Suurmond, *Word and the Spirit at Play: Towards a Charismatic Theology*, London: SCM, 1994, 75–83.

15 Ecclesiastes 3:4.

16 K. Josef Kuschel, *Laughter: A Theological Reflection*, London: SCM, 1994, 84.

17 Luke 5:34–35.

18 And though there are some who attribute the season of fasting to the period of the church, it seems quite clear to me that Jesus places it simply between the cross and the resurrection. For a discussion of this issue as it occurs in Matthew 9:14–17 see F. D. Bruner, *Matthew: A Commentary*, Volume 1, Grand Rapids/Cambridge: Eerdmans, 2004, 425.

19 See I. Stackhouse, 'Catechesis and baptism' in *Forming Christian Habits in Post-Christendom: The Legacy of Alan and Eleanor Kreider*, J.R. Krabill and S. Murray (eds), Harrisonburg: Herald Press, 2011, 106–111.

20 See S.C. Barton, *The Spirituality of the Gospels*, London: SPCK, 1992, 74–83, for an elaboration of this theme as it occurs in Luke, where joy is especially highlighted.

21 1 Peter 1:3–7.

22 D. Bentley Hart, *The Doors of the Sea: Where Was God in the Tsunami?*, Grand Rapids/Cambridge: Eerdmans, 2005, 62.

23 Suurmond, 81.

24 Wittenberg, *The Silence of the Dark Water*, 135.

25 See D. Capps, 'Nervous Laughter: Lament, Death Anxiety, and Humor', in S.A. Brown and P.D. Millar (eds), *Lament: Reclaiming Practices in Pulpit, Pew and Public Square*, Louisville: Westminster John Knox Press, 2007, 70–79.

26 Romans 5:3–5.

27 M. Berman, *The Twilight of American Culture*, New York/London: W.W. Norton, 2000, 106.

Chapter Seven – For the Love of Place

1 See D. Aune, *Revelation: Word Biblical Commentary Series*, Waco: Word, 1992, 108–112.

2   2 Corinthians 3:2.

3   See M. Bunting, *The Plot: A Biography of an English Acre*, London: Granta, 211. She recounts J.B. Priestley's critique of modern England, who argued that so much of modern England 'belonged far more to the age itself than this particular island.'

4   Ibid., 210.

5   See K. Norris, *Dakota: A Spiritual Geography*, New York: Houghton Mifflin, 1993.

6   Psalm 60:7–8.

7   See A. Beckett, *When the Lights Went Out: What Really Happened to Britain in the Seventies*, London: Faber & Faber, 2009, 418–433, for a cultural assessment of new towns, leisure amenities, shopping centres and the violation of place.

8   G. Bernanos, *The Diary of a Country Priest*, London: Fount, 1977, 22–23.

9   Berman, *The Twilight of American Culture*, 88.

10 G.M. Hopkins, 'Binsey Poplars' (1879), in Hopkins, *Poetry and Prose*, 39.

11 For a fuller treatment of this theme see D.A. Hohne, *Spirit and Sonship: Colin Gunton's Theology of Particularity and the Holy Spirit*, Farnham: Ashgate, 2009.

12 Galatians 3:28.

13 John 4:1–26.

14 Acts 8: 26–40.

15 Acts 9:32–43.

16 2 Corinthians 2:12–13.

17 I attribute the phrase 'church as first family' to Rodney Clapp who questions the way in which we reduce the New Testament concept of family to mean the modern nuclear family. See R. Clapp, *Families at the Crossroads: Beyond Tradition and Modern Options*, Downers Grove: IVP, 1993.

18 See J.R. Myers, *The Search to Belong: Rethinking Intimacy, Community, and Small Groups*, Grand Rapids: Zondervan, 2003.

19 Bonhoeffer, *Life Together*, 20.

20 Bonhoeffer, *Life Together*, 22–23.

21 See Pete Ward, *Selling Worship: How What We Sing Has Changed the Church*, Milton Keynes: Authentic, 2005.

22 H. Müller, *The Passport*, transl. M. Chalmers, Exeter: Serpent's Tail, 2009, 63.

22 Bonhoeffer, *Life Together*, 15–16.

Chapter Eight – Passionate Leadership

[1] http://the99percent.com/tips/5679/checkpoints-professionalism

[2] For a convincing critique of the clinical, somewhat impersonal mood of modern psychotherapeutic counselling see J.H. Olthuis, *The Beautiful Risk: A New Psychology of Loving and Being Loved*, Grand Rapids: Zondervan, 2001.

[3] E.H. Peterson, *The Message: The Bible in Contemporary Language*, Colorado Springs: NavPress Publishing Group, 2002.

[4] See D. Hansen, *The Power of Loving Your Church*, Minneapolis: Bethany House Publishers, 1998, 71–74.

[5] For an extended treatment of the maternal imagery in Paul see B.R. Gaventa, *Interpretation: First and Second Thessalonians*, Louisville: John Knox, 1998, 31–34.

[6] For a discussion on the limits of professionalism as related to pastoral care see V. Herrick and Ivan Mann, *Jesus Wept: Reflections on Vulnerability in Leadership*, London: DLT, 1998, 103–116.

[7] 2 Corinthians 3:1–3.

[8] Neuhaus, *Freedom for Ministry*, 65.

[9] For a fuller treatment of this theme see I. Stackhouse, *The Gospel-Driven Church: Retrieving Classical Ministries for Contemporary Revivalism*, Milton Keynes: Authentic, 2004.

[10] V. Thomas, *Future Leader: Spirituality, Mentors, Context and Style for Leaders of the Future*, Carlisle: Paternoster, 1999, 24.

[11] E.H. Peterson, *The Wisdom of Each Other: A Conversation Between Spiritual Friends*, Grand Rapids: Zondervan, 1998, 33.

[12] R. Scruton, *The Uses of Pessimism: And the Danger of False Hope*, London: Atlantic Books, 2010, 36.

[13] Luke 10:2.

[14] Indeed, Richard Dormandy may well be right when he says that Paul was a powerful evangelist and a reluctant pastor, hence the burden he felt about the Corinthians – a burden which, Dormandy argues, drove him to despair. See R. Dormandy, *The Madness of St Paul: How St Paul Rediscovered the Love of God*, Chawton: Redemptorist, 2011, 48.

[15] S. Hauerwas, *Christian Existence Today: Essays on Church, World, and Living in Between*, Grand Rapids: Brazos, 1998, 149–167.

[16] A. Root, *Revisiting Relational Youth Ministry: From a Strategy of Influence to a Theology of Incarnation*, Downers Grove: IVP, 2007, 101.

Root has his own problem with platitudinous Christianity. Youth work, he argues, is replete with phrases like 'Take it to God,' or 'Just keep praying'. But in effect such comments are often used to avoid sharing in the pain and suffering of an adolescent's situation.

[17] Ibid., 96.

[18] See Olthuis, *The Beautiful Risk*, 48.

[19] Philippians 2:5–11.

[20] H. Nouwen, *In the Name of Jesus: Reflections on Christian Leadership*, London: Darton, Longman and Todd, 1989.

Chapter Nine – Untamed Hospitality

[1] *Guildford Magazine*, Jan 2011, 17.

[2] M. Borg, *Jesus: A New Vision*, San Francisco: Harper, 1987, 86–93.

[3] Eagleton, *Reason, Faith, and Revolution*, 23.

[4] Luke 14:12–14.

[5] See E. Newman, *Untamed Hospitality: Welcoming God and Other Strangers*, Grand Rapids: Brazos Press, 2007, 19–40.

[6] Matthew 25:40.

[7] L. Bretherton, *Hospitality as Holiness: Christian Witness Amid Moral Diversity*, Aldershot: Ashgate, 2006.

[8] Ibid., 133.

[9] J. Vanier, *From Brokenness to Community*, New York: Paulist Press, 1992, 20.

[10] Ibid., 19.

[11] H.J.M. Nouwen, *Adam: God's Beloved*, London: DLT, 1997, 40.

[12] For a critique of the 'cult of normalcy' and the way in which disability forces us to recognize our own sense of vulnerability see T.F. Reynolds, *Vulnerable Communion: A Theology of Disability and Hospitality*, Grand Rapids: Brazos Press, 2008.

[13] Nouwen, *Adam: God's Beloved*, 65.

[14] G. Greene, *A Burnt-Out Case*, London: Heinemann, 1960.

[15] B. Byrne, *The Hospitality of God: A Reading of Luke's Gospel*, Collegeville: The Liturgical Press, 2000, 124.

[16] Luke 4:16–21.

[17] See A. Sutherland, *I Was a Stranger: A Christian Theology of Hospitality*, Nashville: Abingdon Press, 2006.

18 See R. Campbell, *How to Really Love Your Child*, New York: David. C. Cook, 2004, 43–76.

19 C. Pohl, *Making Room: Recovering Hospitality as a Christian Tradition*, Grand Rapids/Cambridge: Eerdmans, 1999, 171.

20 See C. Plantinga, *Not the Way It's Supposed to Be: A Breviary of Sin*, for a most provocative expose of the sins of avoidance, as he calls them, cocooning being one of them.

21 Matthew 5:20.

22 McGinley, *Saint Watching*, 22.

23 Ibid., 22–23.

24 Quoted in A. Walker, 'Homiletics and Biblical Fidelity: An Ecclesial Approach to Orthodox Preaching', in *Text Message*, I. Stackhouse and O. Crisp, eds., Eugene: Wipf & Stock, Forthcoming.

Conclusion: Holy the Wild

1 D. Hansen, *A Little Handbook on Having a Soul*, Downers Grove: IVP, 1997, 141.

2 1 Kings 18–19.

3 Genesis 12.

4 Plekon, *Hidden Holiness*, 42.

5 See K. Redfield Jamieson, *Touched with Fire: Manic-depressive Illness and the Artistic Temperament*, New York: The Free Press, 1993.

6 Genesis 22.

7 Luke 7:36–50.

8 K. Barth, *The Word of God and the Word of Man*, transl. D. Horton, London: Hodder and Stoughton, 1928, 38.

9 See W. Brueggemann, *Praying the Psalms: Engaging Scripture and the Life of the Spirit*, Carlisle: Paternoster, 2007, 29–42.

10 M. Oliver, 'A Certain Sharpness in the Morning Air', in *New and Selected Poems*, Volume One, Boston: Beacon Press, 1992, 41.

11 Isaiah 29:13, quoted in Matthew 15:8.

12 See E.F. Davis, 'Teaching the Bible Confessionally in the Church', in E.F. Davis and R.B. Hays (ed.), *The Art of Reading Scripture*, Grand Rapids: Eerdmans, 2003, 18.

13 Bonhoeffer, *Life Together*, 18.

14 Psalm 51:16–17.

15 Hebrews 3:7–8.

[16] Hebrews 4:12–13.

[17] Cited in B. Brock, *Singing the Ethos of God: On the Place of Christian Ethics in Scripture*, Grand Rapids/Cambridge: Eerdmans, 2007, 290.

[18] T.S. Eliot, 'Four Quartets: Burnt Norton' in T.S. Eliot, *Collected Poems: 1909–1962*, London: Faber & Faber, 1963, 190.

[19] Brock, *Singing the Ethos of God*, 293. The doctrine of justification by faith was arrived at, her argues, not by way of Romans but by way of the Psalms.

[20] L. William Countryman, *Lovesongs and Reproaches: Passionate Conversations with God*, 2010, 5.

[21] R. Williams and J. Chittester, *For All That Has Been, Thanks: Growing a Sense of Gratitude*, Norwich: Canterbury Press, 2010, 58.

Epilogue

[1] K.E. Bailey, *Poet and Peasant & Through Peasant Eyes: A Literary-Cultural Approach to the Parables in Luke*, Grand Rapids: Eerdmans, 1983, Volume Two, 1–21.

[2] There are those who would translate this verse to mean that she was forgiven much because she loved much but, as Bailey and others point out, not only is this dubious linguistically, it also goes against the whole tenor of Luke's gospel by intimating that love is a precondition of grace, rather than a consequence of forgiveness.

[3] P. Tillich, *The New Being*, London: SCM, 1963, 10.

Subject and Author Index

Biblical Index

Biblical Index

Understanding Jesus

Five Ways to Spiritual Enlightenment

Peter Williams

Peter Williams examines the Gospel accounts of Jesus' life from an apologetic perspective clearing the ground from pre-conceived ideas and prejudices and opening up five ways to consider the claims of Jesus' life and ministry. Williams encourages readers to take Jesus seriously and gives serious reasons why we should. Understanding Jesus helps readers to make their own informed response to the historical Jesus.

'Aquinas offered five ways to God; Peter Williams gives five powerful reasons for thinking that God revealed Himself in Jesus Christ. While the new atheists recycle nineteenth century doubts about the historicity and divinity of Jesus, Williams appeals to the most recent work of qualified scholars, including secularists and Jewish scholars as well as Christian authorities. He shows the evidence is stronger than ever for the New Testament account of Jesus' life and works, and that Jesus continues to transform lives today – **Angus J.L. Menuge Ph.D., Professor of Philosophy, Concordia University Wisconsin, USA.**

Peter S. Williams is a Christian philosopher and apologist. He is an Assistant Professor in Communication & Worldviews, Gimlekollen School of Journalism and Communication, Kristiansand, Norway.

978-1-84227-739-3

No More Law!

A Bold Study in Galatians

Bruce Atkinson

No More Law! is an accessible commentary on Paul's letter to the Galatian church. In it Bruce Atkinson concentrates on the work of the Holy Spirit in the Christian life; walking in the Spirit, how this brings freedom and produces godliness. He maintains a good theological balance between the Word and the Spirit, the gospel and the place of the Mosaic Law, freedom from that Law, but with an emphasis upon our responsibility to live godly lives in today's world.

'Bruce Atkinson offers a singularly pure treatment on the triumph of grace over law based on the book of Galatians. Powerful and convincing, his written exposition reflects his bold preaching style. *No More Law!* is first Century truth effectively applied to twenty-first Century hearts. A joy to read' – **Colin Dye, Senior Minister of Kensington Temple and a member of the National Leadership Team of the Elim Pentecostal Churches.**

Bruce Atkinson is the Associate Minister of Kensington Temple Elim Pentecostal Church, Notting Hill Gate, London.

978-1-84227-747-8

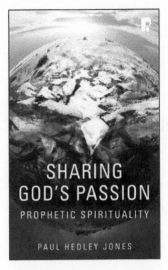

Sharing God's Passion

Prophetic Spirituality

Paul Hedley Jones

This book seeks to illuminate the critical role the prophets played in God's overarching purposes for his creation, and how we in the 21st century may also learn to collaborate with God. *Sharing God's Passion* provides a comprehensive overview of the various dimensions of a prophetic spirituality through a series of fifteen studies, each based on events in the life of the prophets, starting with Moses through to John of Patmos, including two chapters on Jesus, himself. The studies offer in-depth analyses of biblical texts, suggestions for life application, and questions for personal reflection or group discussion.

'Paul Jones has written a persuasive walk through the prophets. His interpretations are reliable, with an eye on the contemporaneity of these old texts. An interesting feature that commends the book is Jones's continuation of the prophetic trajectory into the New Testament' – **Walter Brueggemann, Columbia Theological Seminary**

Paul Hedley Jones is a doctoral student, working under Professor R.W.L. Moberley, at Durham University, UK.

978-1-84227-745-4

Light on Prophecy

Retrieving Word and Prophecy in Today's Church

Jennifer Campbell

The author correlates the vision and thinking of two powerful prophetic leaders: Hildegard of Bingen, a twelfth-century enclosed nun/mystic, and Dietrich Bonhoeffer, the twentieth-century German pastor/theologian executed by the Nazis. With a view to recovering a balanced and rounded theology of prophecy for the church today, she discusses the closely rel-ated workings of both the Word of God (viewed as Christ and the Scriptures) and the Holy Spirit in the works and lives of these famous Christians.

'Rarely do we encounter maturity, depth and wisdom when the subject at hand is the prophetic gift. Jenny Campbell's book is the exception. With rare insight she offers us a workable and thorough theology of Prophecy' – **Mike Breen, 3DM Global Leader.**

Jennifer Campbell is a lecturer in Christian Doctrine at Westminster Theological Centre, Cheltenham, UK. She is also the leader of Eaglesinflight.

978-1-84227-768-3